THE CONSTRUCTION COMPANY IN AND OUT OF RECESSION

The Construction Company in and out of Recession

Patricia M. Hillebrandt
Construction Industry Consultant
Senior Visiting Research Fellow, University of Reading

Jacqueline Cannon
Managing Director
Construction Forecasting and Research Ltd

and

Peter Lansley
Professor of Construction Management
University of Reading

Foreword by N.I. Simms
Group Chief Executive of Tarmac plc

A report on a study sponsored by the
Engineering and Physical Science Research Council

First published 1995 by
MACMILLAN PRESS LTD
Houndmills, Basingstoke, Hampshire RG21 6XS
and London
Companies and representatives
throughout the world

ISBN 0–333–61770–3 hardcover
ISBN 0–333–61771–1 paperback

A catalogue record for this book is available
from the British Library.

10   9   8   7   6   5   4   3   2   1
04 03 02 01 00 99 98 97 96 95

Printed in Great Britain by
Ipswich Book Co Ltd, Ipswich, Suffolk

To our children:
Adrian, Alison, Carolyn, Imogen, John,
Joy, Robert and Robin

10.5	Diversification	159
10.6	International contracting	161
10.7	Financial strategy	162
10.8	Pricing policy	163
10.9	Internal and external markets	163
10.10	Management and organisation structure	165
10.11	Effect of recession on innovation	168
10.12	Conclusion	169

Appendix 1: Changes in Accounting Rules; Exceptional
Items; Extraordinary Items   173

Appendix 2: Location of Discussion of Topics in the
Three Books; Contents of Companion Volume,
'The Management of Construction Firms:
Aspects of Theory'; Contents of Companion Volume,
'The Modern Construction Firm'   175

Subject Index   177

Index of Names   183

Contents

List of Figures   xi

List of Tables   xiii

Foreword   xv

Acknowledgements   xvii

Abbreviations and Acronyms   xix

Introduction   xxi

PART I   THE INDUSTRY

1   The Construction Industry and its Environment   **3**
  1.1   Introduction   3
  1.2   Major influences   6
  1.3   Boom to recession in the economy and in the
        construction industry   11
        1.3.1   Private housing   14
        1.3.2   Commercial construction   17
        1.3.3   Public building   20
        1.3.4   Infrastructure   21
  1.4   Conclusion   23

2   Financial Aspects of Large Construction Companies   **25**
  2.1   Introduction   25
  2.2   Companies' balance sheets   25
  2.3   Turnover and profits   30

PART II   THE CONTRACTORS AND THEIR STRATEGIES

3   Financial Considerations   **37**
  3.1   Introduction   37
  3.2   Capital   37
  3.3   Profits   46
  3.4   Dividends   49
  3.5   Share values   50

3.6		Cash flow	52
	3.6.1	Contracting	52
	3.6.2	Housing	54
	3.6.3	Property	55
	3.6.4	Mining and minerals	56
3.7		Bonding and credit	57
3.8		Financial control within companies	58
3.9		External influences	59

4 Markets and Marketing — **63**

4.1	Introduction	63
4.2	Retreat to core businesses	63
4.3	Contracting	65
4.4	Housing development	66
4.5	Commercial property development	68
4.6	Mining and minerals	69
4.7	International businesses	69
4.8	Marketing policy	73

5 Marketing Contracting Services — **77**

5.1		Introduction	77
5.2		Response of companies to recession	77
5.3		Extension of existing services	78
	5.3.1	Developing regional penetration	78
	5.3.2	Expanding work abroad	80
	5.3.3	Taking over contracts from companies in receivership	80
	5.3.4	Improvement of quality	82
5.4		New services and new ways of supplying existing services	82
	5.4.1	Design and build and other non-traditional contracts	82
	5.4.2	Provision of finance and financial packages	85
	5.4.3	New forms of diversification and specialisation	88
	5.4.4	Links with other contractors	91

6 Structure, Management Methods and Planning — **93**

6.1	Introduction	93

List of Figures

1.1   UK construction output by sector 1983, 1990, 1993   5
1.2   Public and private new construction output 1983–93   8
1.3   Affordability ratio and interest rates 1983–93   12
1.4   Bank lending to construction and property companies 1985–93   13
1.5   Private new construction orders and output 1983–93   13
1.6   Indices of house prices, retail prices, and average earnings 1983–93   15
1.7   Private housing output, orders and starts 1983–9   16
1.8   Private housing output, South East and rest of GB 1988–93   17
1.9a   Private sector housing starts by region 1985, 1989, 1993   18
1.9b   Private commercial output by region 1985, 1989, 1993   18
1.9c   Infrastructure output by region 1985, 1989, 1993   18
1.10   Public and private housing starts 1980–93   21
1.11   New infrastructure orders by type of work 1985–93   22
1.12   New public and private infrastructure orders 1985–93   23
2.1   Net assets of 70 of the top 80 UK construction companies 1988–93   28
2.2   Exceptional items of 70 of the top 80 UK construction companies 1987–93   29
2.3   Turnover of 70 of the top 80 UK construction companies and all contractors' new construction output 1987–93   31
2.4   Turnover by activity of 70 of the top 80 construction companies 1987–93   32
2.5   Pre-tax profits of 70 of the top 80 construction companies 1987–93   33
2.6   Pre-tax profits by activity of 70 of the top 80 UK construction companies 1987–93   34

List of Figures

3.1 Pre-tax profits by activity of 17 companies in
     the survey 1987–93   47
3.2 Pre-tax profits/losses and dividends of 17 companies
     in the survey 1989–93   50
3.3 FTSE Building and construction UK share prices
     1987–94   51
10.1 Extended growth-share portfolio matrix   151
10.2 Industry attractiveness and business strengths matrix   153
10.3 Profitability-business type matrix   154
10.4 Growth-profitability matrix   155

List of Tables

1.1	Number of firms and value of work done in 1987, 1989 and 1993	6
2.1	Eighty top companies	26
2.2	Gearing of sixty top companies	30
3.1	Actions taken in response to recession during the period 1989 to 1993	38
3.2	Exceptional items in balance sheets	41
3.3	Turnover and pre-tax profits/losses of companies in the survey	45
4.1	Core businesses of construction companies	64
5.1	Contracting market-related actions taken in response to recession during the period 1989–93	78
8.1	Responses to the recession: UK industry and construction industry	122
10.1	Reasons for movement to market supply	164
10.2	Propensity to innovate in construction and manufacturing industry	168

Foreword

I was delighted to be asked by the authors to provide a foreword to this book as I was to contribute to their research into what must have been a very demanding subject both intellectually and emotionally. I was only able to presume that in seeking my support they felt that someone who had seen the highest of highs in 1988 and experienced the lowest of lows in 1992 had a unique advantage in reviewing this latest recession in our industry.

In this the third of a series of books on the strategic behaviour of large construction companies, the authors describe how companies have had to fight for survival as their UK markets collapsed in the wake of the sudden tightening of monetary policy in the late 1980s. The impact was first felt in the housing and property markets, and then on the rest of the construction industry, as the severe recession which followed destroyed profitability and caused problems to many balance sheets. The book demonstrates that, as the conditions in the UK construction market changed rapidly from boom to recession, companies, who had assumed that growth would continue indefinitely, were forced to move quickly to reduce debt, reduce costs, reduce employment and restructure to restore balance in their businesses. The results of investing the free cash flow from contracting activities into the cash hungry activities of housebuilding and property development in the second half of the 1980s had to be rapidly redressed.

The body of the book describes how, once the initial repair work had been done, the surviving companies took action in response to the recession by introducing a series of initiatives aimed at rebuilding their businesses by looking for competitive advantage. Corporate planning, or rather the lack of it, is seen as one reason why some companies suffered more than others. There is an important message for the future that companies must continuously monitor what is happening and what is likely to happen in their markets, and set out to manage accordingly. Chapter 8 concludes that there have been major changes in strategy between the authors' survey in 1986 and their follow-up in 1993. The final chapter then explains that many of the theoretical approaches that had been offered to analyse and explain the decision-making processes in large construction companies proved to be irrelevant in a period of crisis and decline. The conclusion is that much research still needs to be done to help future generations of managers avoid the pitfalls which we can now see more clearly with hindsight.

The authors have provided a very useful review of the reasons for and the impact of the recession on the UK construction industry. As such, their new report should be essential reading for all those whose actions impact upon, and those who work in, our industry. An industry that creates approximately 10 per cent of GDP is of sufficient importance to have a place at the top of the national agenda but, once there, it must learn to improve its performance by applying the lessons of the past to the vision for the future. This report makes a useful contribution to that aim.

N.I. SIMMS
Group Chief Executive of Tarmac plc

Acknowledgements

We should like to thank the Engineering and Physical Sciences Research Council for supporting this study and for their encouragement to publish the findings. We are grateful to the construction companies which participated for their willingness to discuss the operation of their organisations and their response to the recession – in many cases dealing openly with sensitive issues. The companies which cooperated in the project are: Balfour Beatty Ltd, Henry Boot & Sons plc, Bovis Construction Ltd, Costain Group plc, Galliford plc, Higgs & Hill plc, Kier Group plc, Kyle Stewart Ltd, John Laing plc, Y J Lovell Holdings plc, Miller Group Ltd, John Mowlem & Co plc, Tarmac plc, Taylor Woodrow plc, Try Group plc, Wilmot Dixon Ltd, Wilson Connolly plc, George Wimpey plc.

We wish to express our thanks to friends, colleagues and family for their encouragement and support through the period of the study, particularly to those who commented on the draft of the book and especially to Jim Meikle who read it not once but several times. We have been greatly helped by the staff at Construction Forecasting and Research Ltd who prepared many of the figures and tables. Lastly the book would not have been possible without the help of Cheryll Joy, who has willingly produced the many successive drafts.

PATRICIA M. HILLEBRANDT
JACQUELINE CANNON
PETER LANSLEY

Abbreviations and Acronyms

BEC	Building Employers Confederation
BS	British Standard
CFR	Construction Forecasting and Research Ltd
CIC	Construction Industry Council
CIEC	Construction Industry Employers Council
CIOB	Chartered Institute of Building
CITB	Construction Industry Training Board
CPD	Continuing professional development
DoE	Department of the Environment
ECGD	Export Credit Guarantee Department
FCEC	Federation of Civil Engineering Contractors
GDP	Gross domestic product
HND	Higher National Diploma
ILO	International Labour Office
INSEAD	European Institute of Business Administration
IT	Information technology
MBA	Master of Business Administration
NEDO	National Economic Development Office
NVQ	National Vocational Qualification
ONC	Ordinary National Certificate
PE	Price/earnings (ratio)
RPI	Retail price index
TUPE	Transfer of Undertaking (Protection of Employment) Regulations 1981
UCATT	Union of Construction and Allied Trades and Technicians
UN	United Nations
VAT	Value added tax

Introduction

This book is the third in a series on the strategic behaviour of large construction companies.The first book, Hillebrandt and Cannon, *The Management of Construction Firms: Aspects of Theory*[1] published in 1989 discussed a number of theoretical approaches from various disciplines as a means to the analysis of decision making processes in major contracting companies. The second book, Hillebrandt and Cannon, *The Modern Construction Firm*,[2] published in 1990 investigated the factors taken into account by large companies in their determination of strategy and the methods of their decision processes during a period of strong economic growth.

This volume seeks to describe the effects of recession on large construction companies. It is clear that the industry has been seriously affected by the downturn in the economy, by the fall in the demands on the industry and by the collapse of the property and housing development markets. It seemed *prima facie* likely that the strategy of the companies in the industry, their organisation and methods of decision making would also have changed. In the disciplines of economics and management it is rarely possible to conduct experiments. The alternative is to take advantage of changes which occur to study their effects. This project took advantage of the downturn to study its effects on the large construction companies. More specifically the purpose of the research was fourfold:

1. to establish how large firms adapted their strategies in response to the recession;
2. to understand the reasons for their responses and to consider the appropriateness of their actions;
3. to find out how they view their future and the changes in the environment in which they operate;
4. to determine how the strategy of firms in boom and in recession relates to theories outlined in the first book and to those developed since.

Investigations for *The Modern Construction Firm* and for this study were carried out by desk research and by interviews with senior

xxi

decision makers in large companies. For this volume interviews with eighteen large companies were carried out in late 1993 and early 1994.

The companies approached responded positively to our request to participate in the study. Some were the same as in the previous study but additional ones were also chosen. All the companies interviewed were in the top 50 of companies by turnover, seven were in the top 10, with sizes ranging from over £100 million turnover to nearly £4000 million. In terms of their financial structure and behaviour they are representative of the larger companies in the construction industry. Most of the companies interviewed were public limited companies. In total there were 13 plcs of which 5 were family controlled or effectively family controlled. Two were subsidiaries of plcs; one was a subsidiary of a foreign company and two were family controlled limited companies. Of the public limited companies interviewed in 1986 about a quarter would have been described as family controlled and another quarter had strong family connections in their management. Since then the influence of families has weakened in the latter group.

Interviews were conducted mostly with main board members or senior executives closely associated with contracting activities. The interviews took the form of free ranging discussions and, while all main subjects were covered, the issues varied from company to company according to their particular concerns. When they were first visited in 1987, all companies were diversified to a greater or lesser extent. Contracting, which in most cases covered both building and civil engineering, was obviously their core business. However some were also strongly involved in process engineering and building services businesses, housing and property development interests in the UK and to some extent, abroad as well. Mining and building materials businesses were also owned by several of them. The same was true for the companies visited in the present study, with the exception of one company which specialised in private sector housing.

The organisation of the book is similar to that adopted in the previous volume. The first chapter compares the differences in the environment of large companies in 1986 and 1993. An appreciation of these differences is essential to a full understanding of the strategic changes adopted by them during the period. Chapter 2 follows the path of the recent development of seventy large companies. This provided an important background for the interviews in the eighteen companies in the study.

The main strategies, which were the focus of the interviews, are discussed in the following six chapters.

Chapter 3 deals with financial considerations and with the abrupt and painful decisions which the recession imposed upon the companies. Chapter 4, on markets, focuses on the retrenchment in their range of activities, the disposal of marginal businesses and on their responses to falling workloads and profits. Chapter 5 analyses the various ways in which they have adapted in order to increase and widen the range of their services in contracting.

Key changes introduced to the structures of the companies, their management methods and approaches to planning are the subject of Chapter 6, while Chapter 7 analyses the impact of the fall in workload on staff levels, and the knock-on effect of widespread redundancies on efficiency levels. Chapter 8 presents a review of the survey, with a particular focus on changes in strategy between 1986 and 1993 and on new corporate objectives.

The major concerns for the future of the industry expressed by the companies are at the core of Chapter 9 which deals with excess capacity, operative employment and the policy and regulatory framework within which they currently work. Finally Chapter 10 reviews how the theory expounded in the earlier book on *The Management of Construction Firms: Aspects of Theory*[3] has stood up to changing conditions. It also comments on some recent developments in theory, highlights some of the areas where change is necessary, and, in some areas, proposes some redevelopment of existing ideas.

Lastly for ease of reference the location of subjects in the earlier two books is compared with their location in this book in Appendix 2.

References

1. Hillebrandt, Patricia M. and Cannon, Jacqueline, *The Management of Construction Firms: Aspects of Theory* (London: Macmillan, 1989)
2. Hillebrandt, Patricia M. and Cannon, Jacqueline, *The Modern Construction Firm* (London: Macmillan, 1990)
3. Hillebrandt and Cannon, 1989, op. cit.

Part I
The Industry

1 The Construction Industry and its Environment

1.1 INTRODUCTION

The behaviour of companies is strongly influenced by the environment in which they operate – first the overall economic and political conditions and secondly the state of the construction industry and the nature of the demands being made upon it. Some of these factors are examined in this chapter.

The areas of operations of the large construction companies are described in detail in the following chapters. They encompass contracting, housing development, property development, mineral extraction and materials production. These are very different businesses. For housing development contractors buy land, putting together land banks which may represent several years' building programmes and developing housing on it to meet anticipated demand. They do not generally undertake the construction themselves but contract it out to smaller builders. The houses are sold to the occupier or where the development is for social housing the houses are sold to a Housing Association or Trust which is responsible for letting them. In the case of property development the construction company may act alone or with others. As in the case of housing the land is purchased and an office or other commercial building is constructed and then let or sold. In some cases the building is prelet, presold or developed in conjunction with the ultimate owner who may be the occupier or an investor. Because most buildings are of little market value until they are let or sold and because of the long construction period the investment at any one time by the construction company is usually larger than in the case of housing. Thus the risks are substantial. Cases of where buildings have appreciated in value more rapidly when empty than when occupied do arise but they are relatively unusual.

In the case of contracting the construction company does not normally invest its own money in the project but undertakes the building or civil work to the order of the client. Risks are less than in property development or housing.

3

Mineral production may be for building materials, notably aggregates of various types, or it may be for materials unrelated to construction such as coal or metals. The latter are not covered in this chapter. The demand for construction-related materials generally follows the demand for construction. It is not specifically discussed in this chapter because it is relatively unimportant in the operations of most construction companies.

All the above activities are influenced by the state of the economy. For example by expectations of clients, rates of interest and the availability of credit. However housing development and property development, largely because of the specific markets which they serve, are also subject to other fluctuations unrelated to the state of the economy. These may arise from, for example, changes in legislation, over-supply due to the long production period or changes in demand for specific reasons such as the 'Big Bang'.

The construction industry undertook £46.3 billion of work in 1993 and 49% of the output in current prices was repair and maintenance. Taking into account that some repair and maintenance work is uncounted, these figures probably understate its importance. Figure 1.1 shows the split of total work into new and repair and maintenance and the types of work undertaken in 1983, 1990 and 1993. Because the data are at 1990 prices they do not reflect the substantial fall in prices from 1990 to 1993.

Because the large construction companies which are the subject of this book undertake mainly new work and some rehabilitation rather than repair and maintenance the data in this chapter refer mainly to new work which, for all except housing, includes rehabilitation work.

The private contracting industry still consists of a relatively small number of large firms undertaking a large proportion of work and a great number of small and medium sized general and specialist contractors and self-employed tradesmen with small workloads. Table 1.1 shows the changes in number of firms and estimates of work done by firms of varying sizes since 1987. The size categories are based on employment and therefore if firms subcontract more work and have fewer direct employees they may go into a smaller size category even though their turnover may not change or may increase. The basis used for estimating value of work done represents work actually carried out by the firms rather than just managed by them and therefore because there is a large amount of subcontracting they are much lower for the large companies than turnover, which in 1993 for the top 70 was nearly £18 billion.

1983

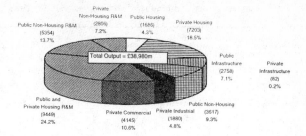

1990

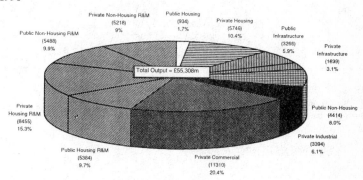

1993

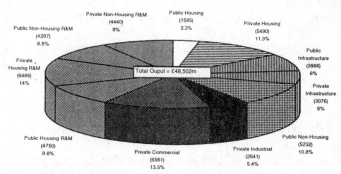

Figure 1.1 UK construction output by sector 1983, 1990, 1993 (£million 1990 prices)

Source: Department of the Environment

Table 1.1   Number of firms and value of work done in 1987, 1989 and 1993

Size of firm (classified by numbers employed)	Number of firms			Estimates of value of work* (£billion current prices)		
	1987	1989	1993	1987	1989	1993
1200 and over	35	48	33	3.7	7.3	4.4
600–1119	71	66	53	2.4	3.4	2.9
300–599	143	153	96	2.3	3.2	2.3
115–299	507	530	330	3.4	4.7	2.5
60–114	849	871	577	2.4	3.5	2.8
25–59	3027	2936	2164	3.7	4.2	4.7
8–24	11 559	10 081	7759	4.4	4.7	4.7
1–7	158 904	86 391	184 095	7.9	10.1	9.9
Total†	175 095	201 076	195 107	30.2	41.2	34.1

*Based on four times the 3rd quarter figures
†Totals do not always sum exactly due to rounding
Source: Based on Department of the Environment statistics.

1.2   MAJOR INFLUENCES

There are five major influences on the behaviour and performance of the construction industry. They are economic and industrial factors, government policy, social and technological changes and external influences; the fifth is the changes which are brought about by the industry itself.

Since the early 1980s considerable changes have occurred in the level of economic activity and also in the structure of the economy. GDP increased by 27% in the decade to 1989. This included a period of recession in the early 1980s and the rapid growth of the late 1980s when it reached 4.5% in one year. After that the rate slowed and GDP actually fell in 1991 and 1992 by 2.3% and 0.5% respectively, with a rise of 0.8% in 1993.

The construction industry both benefitted from the economic growth of the 1980s and contributed to it. The output of the industry, measured in constant 1990 prices, rose by 42% between 1983 and 1990, from £39.0 billion to £55.3 billion and its growth rate reached a peak of 11.5% in 1987. Manufacturing output increased by 26% in the same period with the highest rate of increase in 1988 at 7.1% but the peak of output was in 1989. Consumers expenditure also grew by 33% with the highest rate of increase also in 1988 at 7.5% but the growth continued to a peak in 1990. During the decade there were some interesting changes in the relative size of the major sectors which were either policy or market-led or which reflected shifts in households' behaviour and aspirations.

Business confidence ran high during this period with the banks prepared to lend to businesses both large and small. Foreign investors were also impressed with the boom in the economy and were keen to participate in it with their investment funding rising substantially.

The impact of developments in information technology (IT) was a striking feature of the 1980s and they continue to affect all aspects of working and leisure life. IT implies that a heavy concentration of services employment in London is no longer essential. In the period 1990–93 it is estimated that employment in London decreased by around 250,000 most of which was in the service and retail distribution sectors.

Historically government has been the major client of the construction industry and one of the main changes in the 1980s was the relative reduction in the role of central government, local authorities and other public organisations. Since then public construction output has increased both in relative and absolute terms. By 1993 it had the same share of new work as in 1983, partly because of the fall in private work from 1991 (see Figure 1.2).

The major reason for the change in the role of the public sector as client was the privatisation of the water, sewerage and energy industries in England and Wales but this has been more than offset by increased capital spending of the privatised agencies and expenditure generated by the award of regional and structural funds by the European Union. In addition, these changes coincided with the imposition of very stringent directives on the quality of water from the European Union.

The role of the public sector as client of the industry would have been greater without privatisation, without the determination of government to reduce the proportion of capital spending in the economy and the budget deficit and without the reduction in defence spending in the wake of the dramatic political changes in Europe.

It is not only as a client that the government has reduced its role but also in its support for the development of the industry for example in research and development, and in traditional education and training for the industry. This continued the trend of the 1970s when government

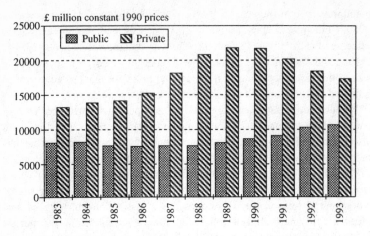

Figure 1.2   Public and private new construction output 1983–93
Source: Department of the Environment.

steadily reduced its involvement in improving the efficiency of the
industry. Contractors generally accept that the industry can no longer
rely on government to help smooth cycles in demand, to solve the industry's problems and to subsidise certain activities. This change in contractors' attitudes has been fostered by a younger generation of top
executives who can barely remember the interventionist era in which the
older members of the industry developed. Whilst there is still concern at
government action it is less about the work available from government
and much more about what is considered the inadequacies of the regulatory framework in which companies can operate effectively.

However very recently government has once more become involved in
consideration of the performance of the industry. There is a mechanism
for these problems to be discussed due to the recent changes in the structure of the sponsorship role of government. After several years of non-
involvement the government is once more participating in debate about
research, education and training and contractual arrangements. During
1993 the Department of the Environment (DoE) became more open,
receptive and proactive, initiated wide ranging discussions with industry
at several levels and has contributed funds and ideas to relevant research
projects including the Latham Report[1] and the Private Finance Initiative.

It is adopting a 'Whole Industry Research Strategy' and is reviewing construction statistics. The immediate fruits of the new approach are a better understanding by the industry and by the Department of each other's major concerns and priorities. It remains to be seen whether in the longer term, this leads to greater efficiency of the industry.

A number of fundamental social changes are taking place and the pace of these changes increased in the 1980s. Some of them, although demographic in character, are actually due to technological developments, for example improved health care and longer life. Changes in employment patterns include more women at work, more part-time work, gradually, more home-based work and earlier retirement. The effect on construction of social changes includes more housing for single persons and single parents, more special needs housing, especially for older retired households and for those in need of care. However the bulk of private housing is still for conventional families. More criminal behaviour has created a need for construction of prisons.

Technological changes have also affected the share of work undertaken by main contractors and specialist subcontractors with the development of sophisticated buildings such as offices, hospitals, prisons and, more recently, high-bay warehouses so that the share of the higher value-added building services in construction costs rose considerably. However, these may now be decreasing with mounting concern for the environment and the high cost of buildings.

Directives from the European Union have affected the spending on utilities and infrastructure in the UK, as have regional and structural fund grants. They have also increased opportunities for the UK industry and affected the way in which the construction industry functions in terms of competitive behaviour by contractors and professionals and will have further impact in terms of liability and standards. The building materials industry has perhaps been affected more than the contracting industry especially in the run-up to the Single Market because of changes in specifications and standards, opening the whole community to competition and opportunities for more rational distribution systems. There have been more links between large companies across country borders than previously and these have facilitated the construction of mega-projects such as the Channel Tunnel and the second Severn crossing. At the same time European Union initiatives and funding have fostered very large projects across Europe in which a number of large UK contractors have participated.

Recent changes in the world political situation, with the break up of the regimes in Eastern Europe and the ending of the cold war, have meant that defence capital expenditure has changed in terms of type of project but it remains considerable.

The UK industry has always had strong international interests. During the boom it neglected overseas markets but since 1989 has made strong efforts to obtain more work abroad. At the same time, several countries have broken through the growth barrier and the rate of increase of their GDP is substantial. Large sums are being spent on major infrastructure projects which are open to international bidding although the number of countries operating internationally has also increased. South East Asia has replaced the Middle East as a major source of work for the UK construction industry.

There have been changes in the UK construction industry itself due to changes in the relationship between major contractors and large and sophisticated private clients of the industry who give more emphasis to quality and speed than public clients. This is in contrast to the European Union directives and government legislation and guidelines which require the award of the contract to the tenderer offering the best value for money, often interpreted as the lowest bid. During the 1980s the ways of organising the construction process continued to diversify.

Regrettably the pressures on the industry from within and from without in the 1980s and 1990s have not yet led to any reduction in the number of representative bodies. It is claimed that too many of them are still fighting for their own interests rather than working together and that the modernisation of the construction industry is still hampered by the fragmentation of its representative bodies. At the same time, four umbrella bodies have been set up in the past few years with a number of actual and potential future benefits for the industry. They are the Construction Industry Council (CIC) which brings together professional organisations, the Construction Industry Employers Council (CIEC), made up of those which represent contractors and the Construction Liaison Group for specialist subcontractors. The latest proposal is to set up an organisation which would represent the interests of major contractors by merging BEC and FCEC. It would be a member of CIEC.

The long standing problems of the construction industry have been analyzed in a report jointly commissioned by the Government and the industry from Sir Michael Latham, published in the summer of 1994 under the title: *Constructing the Team*.[2] This reviewed the procurement and contractual arrangements in the industry as well as problems such as training, education and research and development. It would be fair to say that there is little new in the issues which need tackling and that the ultimate success of the report lies only in how well its recommendations are implemented. As is noted in the Executive Summary to the Latham Report 'previous reports on the construction industry have either been implemented incompletely or the problems have persisted. The opportunity which exists now must not be missed', hence a proposal for the establishment of an 'Implementation Forum' to advise a Standing Strategic Group of the Construction Industry, chaired by the Secretary of State and with members drawn from the major groups representing contractors and, importantly, clients.

1.3   BOOM TO RECESSION IN THE ECONOMY AND IN THE CONSTRUCTION INDUSTRY

The recession which developed from the autumn of 1988 had its origins in the lax monetary policy of the previous years. Lending institutions, no longer controlled by the Bank of England, fuelled consumer spending so that credit rose to unprecedented levels. Rapid rises in salaries in the South East, combined with lower levels of taxation, considerably increased real purchasing power. Confidence was buoyed by house price rises which induced a feeling of increasing wealth and by expectations of continuing house price increases at a rate greater than the retail price index (RPI). The RPI was itself rising and the percentage increase reached double figures in 1990. In order to counteract the runaway boom in the late 1980s there was a strong reversal of monetary policy with a doubling of interest rates from 7.5% to 15% in the space of seventeen months. Mortgage rates rose in line with interest rates generally so that housing costs for many households nearly doubled and affordability fell dramatically (see Figure 1.3).

Figure 1.4 shows bank lending to construction and property companies between 1985 and 1993. Whereas bank lending to construction companies more than trebled from 1985 to 1990, lending to property companies increased fivefold. The reduction since then has been relatively modest. This amount of bank lending was to have dramatic consequences for the industry in the next few years.

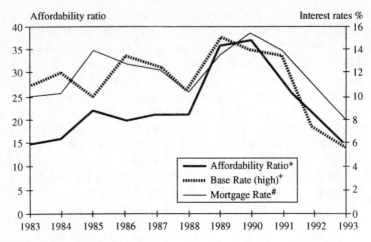

Figure 1.3   Affordability ratio and interest rates 1983–93
* Affordability ratio is based on the first year mortgage interest payment as a %
of two income household post tax earnings
+ Mortgage rate is that of the first quarter for each year
# Base rate is the high for each year
Sources: House Builders Federation, *Housing Market Report, Economic
Trends.*

The recession in the construction industry began in 1988 in one sector
only, namely, housing. Other private building sectors, particularly
offices, fell prey to the rapid increases in financing costs which posed a
serious threat to the viability of many projects especially because there
was so great an over-supply of offices. Figure 1.5 shows new orders and
output for housing, commercial and industrial building and infrastructure. Generally the lags between orders and output were short for
housing and industrial building but in commercial building orders
peaked a year earlier than output because of the large size of projects.
There were dramatic falls in housing output from 1988 and in commercial output from 1990. Changes in industrial building were less dramatic.
Infrastructure was much influenced by the Channel Tunnel and investment by the privatised water and energy industries.

Repair and maintenance work which grew from 1981 through to 1990,
suffered a heavier percentage loss between then and 1993 (19%) than

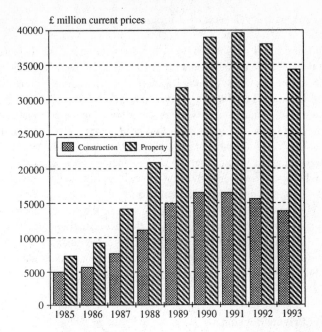

Figure 1.4 Bank lending to construction and property companies 1985–93
Source: Bank of England.

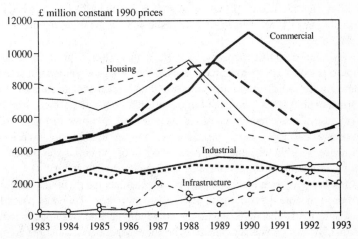

Figure 1.5 Private new construction orders and output 1983–93
Note: Orders shown in broken lines
Source: Department of the Environment.

new work with a 7% decline. Both are shown in 1990 prices in Figure 1.1.

Building, civil engineering and building services had all benefited from the rapid increase in demand for construction. Building contractors and building services companies shared in the private construction boom, while civil engineering contractors saw infrastructure work more than double. When the downturn came its impact permeated right through the firms of the industry, but large companies felt it rapidly as tenders for large commercial projects dried up at the same time as their housebuilding businesses were in dire financial straits. They responded by tendering for a wider and lower value range of projects, thus squeezing the market of medium size contractors.

Over the period, as output grew, the size of the workforce remained relatively stable at around 1.5 million, then rose sharply from 1987 to a peak of 1.8 million in 1990 from which it has since fallen to an estimated 1.4 million in 1993. About 49% of the workforce is in contracting, 11% in public authorities and 40% are self employed.

1.3.1   Private housing

The rise in house prices with high expectations for continuing increases and substantial income growth were major factors in the boom in housebuilding until 1988. Figure 1.6 below shows how these factors are interrelated.

Average earnings were rising more than the retail price index but house prices to 1989 were increasing faster. These developments combined with rapidly mounting interest rates meant that the boom was unsustainable. This is reflected in the affordability ratio, which is based on house prices, interest rates and income levels, shown in Figure 1.3. Average earnings were increasingly lagging behind house prices. However, the factor which triggered the end of the boom was a change in government policy on multiple mortgage house ownership.

For some years it had been possible for each person owning a share in a house to obtain taxation relief on their mortgage. This was patently unfair to married couples where the tax relief was limited to one income earner. A change was announced with the Budget of March 1988 to the effect that mortgage tax relief was to be attached to the dwelling, not the person, so that on each house only one person could receive tax relief.

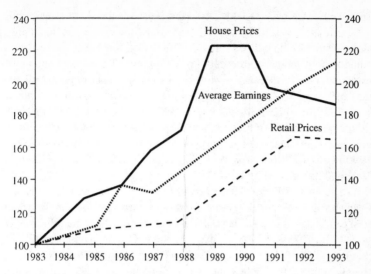

Figure 1.6 Indices of house prices, retail prices and average earnings 1983–93
Source: Nationwide – *House Prices in 1994.*

However implementation was postponed till August 1988 which led to a mad rush by young single people to buy with the benefit of multiple tax relief. This obviously accelerated the rise in house prices as all purchases had to be completed in a strictly limited period. It was during this period that interest rates were at the low level of 8%. After August, and exacerbated by the rise in interest rates, the house market collapsed with transactions falling by unprecedented amounts – over 13% in the fourth quarter 1988 and by 36% from the third quarter 1988 to third quarter 1989. Prices actually fell only from the fourth quarter 1989. The impact of the fall in house prices on the owners and would-be owners was dramatic and its likely long-term effects are still not fully understood. It reduced assumed wealth and left a very large number of home owners with negative equity. Confidence evaporated. The effect on consumer spending, especially on consumer durables was serious and deepened the recession.

The collapse of the housing market left housebuilders with considerably overvalued land banks as the fall in house prices had an immediate knock-on effect on the price of land. From an average of £112 000 per hectare in England in 1981 it rose to a peak of £461 000 in 1988 and by

1994 had fallen back to £401 000. However the number of transactions fell from 1988 to 1991 by 75%. At the same time, where the land banks and the stock of houses were financed by loans, the rise in interest rates considerably increased the cost of borrowings. The disappearance of sales and the adverse cash flow inevitably led a number of housebuilders into bankruptcies. Figure 1.7 shows that the number of private house starts fell from a peak of 221 000 in 1988 to a low of 121 000 in 1992. Starts rather than completions are an indicator of how housebuilders view the future market. The value of output of private housebuilding in 1990 prices fell from a peak of £9.6 billion in 1988 to £5.0 billion in 1991 and then rose slightly to 1993.

The steepest fall in value of private housing output was in the South East, shown by Figure 1.8. From 1988 to 1989 private starts in the South East fell by about a third and in 1992 were less than half that of the peak year. From 1988 to 1992 the fall in the South East accounted for 42% of the total fall for Great Britain. The share of the South East in the Great Britain total at the 1988 peak was a third but by 1992 was about a quarter. This is now less than the proportion of population in the South East which in 1991 was 30% of that of Great Britain.

Figure 1.9a shows the regional[3] distribution of private sector housing starts at four year intervals 1985, 1989 and 1993. The continued domi-

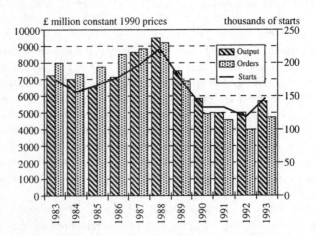

Figure 1.7   Private housing output, orders and starts 1983–93
Source: Department of the Environment.

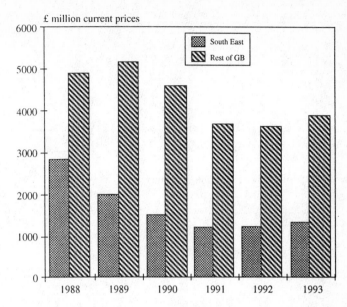

£ million current prices

Figure 1.8 Private housing output; South East and Rest of GB 1988–93
Source: Department of the Environment.

nance of the South East is obvious, as is the fall in its relative importance.

To some extent housebuilders' precarious situation was improved by the Housing Market Package by which the government made £570 million available to Housing Associations for the acquisition of housing in the latter half of 1991/92. Housebuilders were thus able to reduce somewhat the excessive stocks with which they were then burdened. They have continued to develop on behalf of Housing Associations to fill the gap in the demand from households.

1.3.2   Commercial construction

The collapse of the housing market was swiftly followed by that of the commercial property market in London. The feverish office construction boom which developed from 1983 resulted in many more offices under

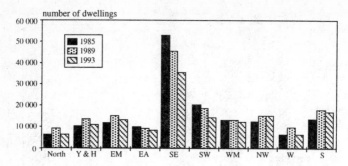

Figure 1.9a   Private housing starts by region 1985, 1989, 1993

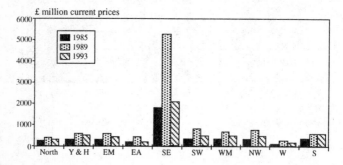

Figure 1.9b   Private commercial output by region 1985, 1989, 1993

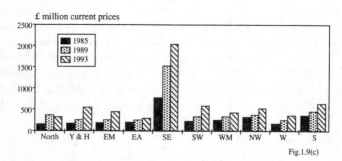

Figure 1.9c   Infrastructure output by region 1985, 1989, 1993
Source: Construction Forecasting and Research Ltd based on Department of the Environment statistics.

construction and completed than were required. However, because of the over optimistic assessments and the long duration of the construction of some office projects, the boom could not be brought swiftly under control. Interest rates climbed to alarming levels and developers, including some major contractors, rushed to complete projects so that they could dispose of them. Banks issued threats of foreclosures as deadlines for settlement of interest charges and repayments were missed. Property investors fled from the market.

The extent of the collapse, which affected London and the South East severely, is clearly illustrated in Figure 1.9b. In 1989 the South East accounted for 55% of commercial construction in Great Britain though it had only 30% of the population. Greater London in 1989 accounted for 58% of commercial building in the South East. The growth in office accommodation in London in particular was greatly in excess of likely demand over the next few years and it will be some time before the oversupply is brought down to levels at which new developments find a suitable array of backers, although outside London recovery will be quicker.

By 1993 orders for offices in current prices were only 28% of their level in 1989 while retail construction in 1993 was 61% of 1989 levels. Retail premises and offices in 1989 accounted for 74% of orders for private commercial construction but by 1993 had fallen to 63%. In 1989 the value of office orders was two and a half times retail orders but by 1993 was only 13% above that of retail.

The development programmes of major food retailers have been the backbone of retail construction for a number of years. They contributed to the growth of the sector throughout the boom and prevented a more catastrophic drop at the time when retail developments generally fell through the floor. Nevertheless, the heavy fall in retail construction brought orders in current prices in 1992 down to £1.0 billion, half what they were in 1989.

Retail developers increased considerably in number in the mid-1980s, with the ranks of traditional operators joined by retailers and financial institutions. The downturn itself reflected the impact of the swift increase in interest rates which together with slower growth of incomes and of consumers' expenditure made tenants for new or yet-to-be completed developments even harder to get.

1.3.3 Public building

Both public housing and public building excluding housing are small by comparison with the corresponding private sectors. Figure 1.10 shows public sector housing compared with private sector housing starts from 1980 to 1993. As in Figure 1.7, starts are quoted rather than completions because they show housebuilders' views of the market.

It will be seen that during the boom to 1988 in private housing, public housing starts were low and falling in absolute as well as relative terms. With the collapse of the private market from 1989, public sector starts continued at a low absolute level and only rose in 1992 and 1993 because of the increase in housing association activity. By 1993 housing association starts accounted for 95% of public sector starts compared with 32% in 1981 and 52% in 1989. This change is due both to a fall in local authority housing to almost negligible levels from 1989 onwards and a rise in housing association starts which more than doubled from 1990, as government funding rose significantly and private finance became more readily available to housing associations with strong balance sheets.

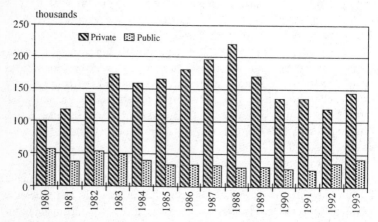

Figure 1.10 Public and private housing starts 1980–93
Source: Department of the Environment.

Public building other than housing consists of a great variety of building types but the dominant ones are educational and health buildings which, in the mid 1980s, accounted for 37% of the total and by 1993 for about 50% of the total. Education orders and output have risen very sharply since 1989. In 1989 contractors output in current prices was £580 million and had risen by 1993 to £1081 million. Although schools and colleges account for two thirds of the total, it is universities which have experienced the highest growth rate, increasing by over three and a half times at current prices since 1989 to cope with the large increase in student numbers. Thus the work in the education sector rose just at the time when private sector construction was decreasing and was helpful in cushioning the effects of the recession.

By contrast health orders peaked in 1989, although output at current prices did not fall until 1993 at current prices. Thus this sector too has had a stabilising effect on output.

Public non-housing building work as a whole kept fairly constant during the boom until 1989 when it started an increase which continued until 1993. Without the positive developments in this sector the fall in contractors' output would have been greater.

1.3.4 Infrastructure

The orders and output series for infrastructure now available show the very rapid increase in the volume of work of the sector since 1987 (see Figure 1.5). While all other types of work were decreasing, infrastructure construction was increasing. This is due to a swift rise in activity by the private sector from 1987 when the order for the Channel Tunnel was released and later, following privatisation, of water and energy utilities.

Whereas public utilities had for many years been starved of capital funds, their privatisation entailed agreements with government which guaranteed considerable increases in capital expenditure. In the case of water and sewerage services compliance with increasingly tight European Union directives has required major investments by water companies which will comfortably exceed £30 billion by the end of the century.

The construction of gas fired power stations and investment in communication networks have also given private infrastructure construction a very strong boost. Orders for major types of work from 1985 to 1993 in current prices are shown in Figure 1.11. They are very erratic because of the influence of mega projects. The relative shares of public and private infrastructure construction are shown in Figure 1.12. The latter clearly illustrates the rapidly rising value of infrastructure orders for the private sector in recent years.

Figure 1.9c above shows infrastructure output by region. Whereas for housing and commercial building the dominance of the South East has lessened, for infrastructure it has increased with investment in the South East in 1993 about triple that of 1985. Much of this includes the effects of the Channel Tunnel which not only itself created a large workload but also generated associated work such as the extension to Waterloo Station. Apart from water and sewerage work, which affected all regions, the South East also benefited from considerable activity in road construction.

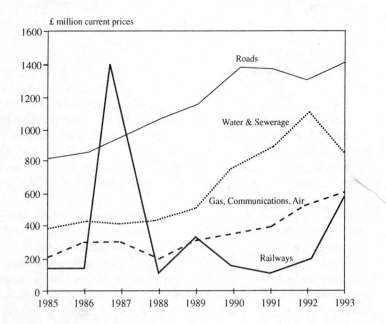

Figure 1.11   New infrastructure orders by type of work 1985–93
Source: Department of the Environment.

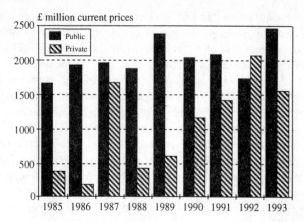

Figure 1.12   New public and private infrastructure orders 1985–93
Source: Department of the Environment.

1.4   CONCLUSION

Through its impact on the housing and property markets, as well as directly on the construction industry, the sudden tightening of monetary policy in 1988 was the main trigger for the recession which has afflicted the industry since then. The housing collapse was itself caused by the high interest rates and the extraordinary decision of the Chancellor to announce mortgage taxation changes months in advance of implementation. Similarly the timing of the collapse of the property market was a result of the rapid rise in interest rates but it was inevitable because of the build-up of so large an oversupply. Thus the construction sector played an unusually significant role in the recession in the economy. The collapse in housing led to a decline in sales of consumer durables and that in property caused large scale bankruptcies which had knock-on effects on the whole economy.

Although construction investment is one of the easiest and earliest expenditure items to cut, in fact, even when investment has been reduced, it may be a long time before the output of the industry falls significantly. This is especially true of the workload of large companies because they are mostly engaged in large long-duration projects. Subcontractors engaged in work at the front end of contracts tend to suffer first. Similarly at the end of a recession it takes a long time for the rise in new orders to translate into workload. The industry is, in mid 1994, just at the point where orders are beginning to increase but output is still depressed. The effect of the past low workload is still keeping margins depressed but they are likely to move up as the orders increase.

While the major contractors were understandably aggrieved by the effects of the recession on their companies, there have been undeniable gains by society during the three years to 1993. Intense competition for work enabled clients to obtain cheaper buildings of good quality, in a shorter time and on conditions suitable to them. The disadvantages of this intense competition are that the industry has neither time nor resources to innovate, educate and train. In the medium to long-term the results will be that the construction process is less efficient, the product possibly of poorer quality, and the industry's competitiveness vis-à-vis foreign firms will be emaciated.

References

1. Latham., M., *Constructing the Team* (London: HMSO, 1994).
2. Ibid.
3. The regions are:– North – North of England; Y & H – Yorkshire and Humberside; EM – East Midlands; EA – East Anglia; SE – South East England; SW – South West England; WM – West Midlands; NW – North West; W – Wales; S – Scotland.

2 Financial Aspects of Large Construction Companies

2.1 INTRODUCTION

Later chapters in this book examine in detail the behaviour and strategies of those companies which participated in the research project. In order to place these firms in perspective it is necessary first to consider the situation of large construction companies in general. Data on seventy of the top eighty companies by turnover have been analysed to obtain information on changes in their turnover, profits, assets, gearing and other financial indicators over the period from 1987 – a year at the earlier stages of the boom – to 1993 when the signs of recovery were first becoming evident. Eighty of the top companies are shown in Table 2.1. They are not necessarily all the top eighty companies because for some there are inadequate data, for example due to being subsidiaries of foreign companies. In the analysis in this chapter only 70 of these have generally been included because for others (mainly smaller companies) 1993 data were not available.

2.2 COMPANIES' BALANCE SHEETS

Almost all the large construction companies had problems with their balance sheets due partly to the collapse of the property and housing markets linked to the over-borrowing of the late 1980s.

Figure 2.1 shows that after a rise in 1989, net assets of the large contractors fell. This was due to the disposal of businesses at values below previous valuations and also the writing-down of land and property assets. The figure shows that at current prices in 1992 and 1993 the value of net assets dipped below the 1988 levels. The change in net assets is linked to the large increase in exceptional items which include write-downs of land and property.

Figure 2.2 shows that, from nil in 1988, exceptional items increased by 1992 to over £900 million for the seventy large companies. The figures for 1993 are based on the new accounting standard FRS3 and

25

Table 2.1 Eighty top companies

Company	£million current prices		
	Turnover		
	1991	*1992*	*1993*
Allen plc	67	59	52
AMEC plc	2338	2122	2184
Amey Holdings Ltd	145	165	214
Balfour Beatty Ltd	1900	1881	1831
Barratt Developments plc	466	438	405
Beazer Homes plc	313	251	276
Bellway plc	108	130	147
Bellwinch plc	21	23	16
Berkeley Group plc	100	126	182
Birse Group plc	317	356	328
Biwater Ltd	263	260	259
Bloor Holdings Ltd	105	125	126
Boot (Henry) & Sons plc	130	129	165
Bovis Construction Ltd	582	460	366
Bovis Homes Ltd	201	173	223
Bryant Group plc	283	323	310
Cala plc	93	66	69
Carter (RG) Holdings Ltd	99	95	94
Charles Church Dev'ts plc	73	33	22
Clugston Group plc	106	94	93
Costain plc	1316	1273	1105
Countryside Properties plc	87	80	92
Crest Nicholson plc	324	238	273
Croudace Ltd	90	67	55
Donelon Tyson plc	81	64	72
EBC Group plc	60	54	58
Eleco Holdings plc	57	45	48
Eve Group plc	47	39	53
Fitzpatrick plc	65	63	60
GA Holdings Ltd	108	94	76
Galliford plc	225	213	217
Gleeson (MJ) Group plc	199	183	168
Haymills Holdings Ltd	100	82	64
Higgs & Hill plc	345	296	262
Jackson Group plc	60	58	61
Jarvis (J) & Sons plc	120	92	71
Johnston Group plc	120	117	127
Keepmoat Holdings Ltd	44	48	54

Table 2.1   continued

Company	£million current prices Turnover		
	1991	1992	1993
Keller Group Ltd	114	132	148
Kier Group plc	614	545	512
Laing (John) plc	1587	1270	1264
Longley (James) Hold's Ltd	81	54	–
Lovell (YJ) Holdings plc	363	275	221
Mansell (R) Ltd	126	101	126
Maunders (John) Group plc	54	52	60
May Gurney Group Ltd	85	84	73
McAlpine (Alfred) plc	621	561	621
McCarthy & Stone plc	73	71	71
Miller Group Ltd	238	258	358
Morrison Construction Ltd	172	193	208
Mowlem (John) & Co plc	1386	1237	1269
Newarthill plc	464	268	231
Norwest Holst Ltd	286	332	295
Osborne (Geoffrey) Ltd	89	83	80
Persimmon plc	144	144	169
Pochin's plc	39	33	47
Prowting plc	41	36	35
Raine Industries plc	352	364	446
Redrow Group Ltd	109	120	130
Roberts (Thomas) West Ltd	48	55	51
Roland Bardsley (Builders) Ltd	41	38	42
Seddon Group Ltd (est.)	76	69	67
Shanks & McEwan plc	118	146	148
Shepherd Building Group Ltd (est.)	387	280	300
Simons Group Ltd	113	116	123
Sunley Turriff Holdings Ltd	89	111	114
Tarmac plc	3225	2935	2669
Tay Homes plc	71	76	70
Taylor Woodrow plc	1395	1245	1150
Tilbury Douglas Ltd	240	382	361
Trafalgar House plc	3089	3890	3879
Try Group plc	114	118	124
Wain Group plc	45	49	57
Ward Holdings plc	30	30	41
Wates Building Group Ltd (est)	240	198	189
Westbury plc	171	132	133

Table 2.1   continued

	£million current prices		
Company	Turnover		
	1991	*1992*	*1993*
Willmot Dixon Ltd (est)	158	152	191
Wilson Bowden plc	136	128	185
Wilson Connolly plc	198	201	274
Wiltshier plc (est)	230	206	209
Wimpey (George) plc	1690	1639	1587
Total	**30 098**	**28 823**	**28 610**

Source: Company accounts.

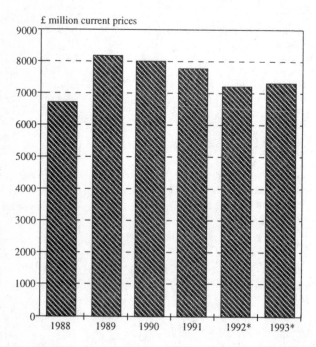

Figure 2.1 Net assets of 70 of the top 80 UK construction companies 1988–93
*The values shown for 1992 and 1993 are based on FRS3 and are therefore not comparable with previous years
Source: Construction Forecasting and Research Ltd based on company accounts.

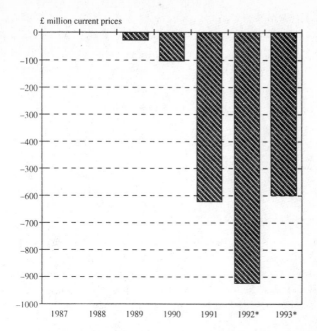

£ million current prices

Figure 2.2 Exceptional items of 70 of the top 80 UK construction companies
1987–93
* The values shown for 1992 and 1993 are based on FRS3 and are therefore not
comparable with previous years
Source: Construction Forecasting and Research Ltd based on company accounts.

definitions for that year differ from those of previous years (see
Appendix 1). However the changes do not invalidate the general conclusion that the losses and the sales of business were concentrated in
the years 1991 and 1992 and had largely been absorbed by 1993.

Gearing, or the debt to equity ratio, shows extraordinary diversity
amongst the large contractors. In 1992 when gearing peaked, it ranged
from nil to over 400% and for nearly half the companies for which
comparable data are available it was considerably higher than in 1988.
In *The Modern Construction Firm*[1] it was reported that some contractors regarded anything over 50% as worrying. Clearly by 1992 a large
number of companies were vulnerable.

Table 2.2 shows gearing of sixty large companies for which comparable data are available.

In 1988 ten companies had nil gearing, in 1989 eleven and in 1992
nine. At the other end there was a dramatic increase in those with over

Table 2.2   Gearing of sixty top companies

Year	Gearing of 5% and less	Gearing of over 5% to under 50%	Gearing of 50% and over
	Number	Number	Number
1988	23	33	4
1989	20	34	6
1992	19	27	14

Source: Construction Forecasting and Research Ltd based on company accounts.

50% gearing. Of these one in 1988, one in 1989 and two in 1992 had gearing of over 300%. However, since 1992 many companies have reduced their gearing (see Chapter 3). Also Table 2.2 understates the change in the industry because five of those companies with high gearing ratios in 1988 had gone out of business by 1992.

2.3   TURNOVER AND PROFITS

About 65% of the turnover of large construction companies is in contracting, the remainder being housing, property development, materials and other. Figure 2.3 shows how total turnover has changed at current prices from 1987 to 1993. Construction prices rose from 1987 to 1990 but actually fell by 18% from 1990 to 1993 so that in real terms turnover has increased steadily.

It is amazing that the level of turnover of the large contractors actually rose during the recession. The figure compares turnover with DoE output of new work at current prices. The two sets of data do not refer to exactly the same types of work. In particular the contractors' turnover includes overseas work, process plant engineering and often property, materials and other businesses, while DoE figures refer only to domestic building and infrastructure output. However, in spite of these differences, it is apparent that the share of the market taken by the large contractors increased at the expense of the smaller ones. DoE

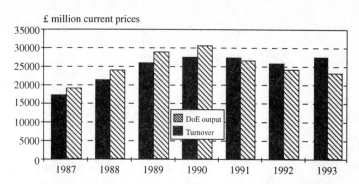

£ million current prices

Figure 2.3 Turnover of 70 of the top 80 UK construction companies and all contractors new construction output 1987–93
Source: Construction Forecasting and Research Ltd based on company accounts and Department of the Environment statistics.

output of new work in current prices fell by 24% from 1990 to 1993. The turnover of the seventy contractors fell only by 0.7% from 1990 to 1991, by 3.1% to 1992 and then rose by 0.7%. While from 1987 to 1990 there was a substantial difference between the two series, in 1991 the gap narrowed. In 1992 the large contractors turnover overtook the DoE output figures and was even higher in 1993. Figure 2.4 shows turnover by types of activity of the 70 large construction companies. This diagram shows a continuing rise in turnover in contracting at current prices. As prices were falling in the latter part of that period the turnover actually increased even more at constant prices.

The major contractors have increasingly become managers of construction and construction related activities rather than undertaking the actual construction of the building or works. This applies in their contracting activities where the amount of subcontracting has steadily increased. Information on the amount of work actually carried out by the large contractors is given in Table 1.1. Precise interpretation of the work done is difficult because of changes in number of firms in each category and because of the difficulty of converting from current to constant prices. However it is reasonable to deduce that there has been

£ million current prices

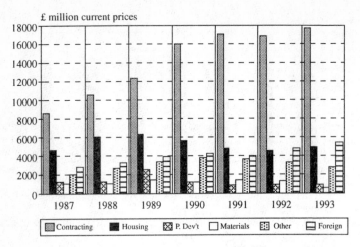

Figure 2.4   Turnover by activity of 70 of the top 80 UK construction companies 1987–93
Source: Construction Forecasting and Research Ltd based on company accounts.

a decrease in the volume of work actually done by large contractors. It also seems likely from the table that they have been subcontracting to firms employing fewer than 60 persons.

The fall in turnover of contractors' other businesses is more marked but still not as great at might be expected given the recession. The figure shows that housing fell from 1989 to 1992 but rose in 1993. Property development in 1993 was over 70% of the levels of pre-1989. The longest continuous decline was in 'other'. The main reason for these falls is that contractors had sold businesses in these areas. This is discussed in more detail for the 18 companies studied in Chapter 4.

Where then is the effect of the recession on the large contractors? It is only necessary to look at the data on profits to find some of the causes.

Unfortunately for this analysis there are problems in interpretation of the data for the year 1993. This is the first year in which the new accounting standards have been implemented and, while turnover figures have not been affected, the basis for the calculation of profit has been altered. Much of the change arises from the different treatment of exceptional items. The effect of the changed rules on profits has been to increase the loss of the large companies from £702 million to £854 million in 1992, a rise of 21.6%.

No change in the statistical basis can mask the disastrous losses of the large contractors in 1991, 1992 and 1993 as shown by Figures 2.5 and 2.6. The largest ones were in housing and property development and the miscellaneous 'other' category. This however does not show the full picture because pre-tax profits include exceptional items such as property and housing land write-offs. These are shown in Figure 2.2. Contracting never actually showed a loss but the fall in profit was very serious and 1993 profits showed no improvement over 1992 levels (See Figure 2.6). On the revised basis the pre-tax profit for 1991 would have been considerably greater (see Figures 2.5 and 2.2). Of thirty three companies which were making losses in 1992 (as restated under FRS3) most

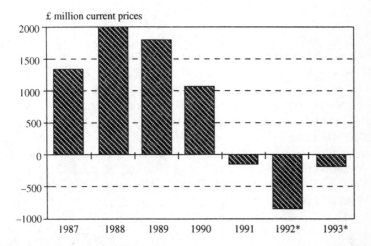

Figure 2.5 Pre-tax profits of 70 of the top 80 construction companies 1987–93
*The values shown for 1992 and 1993 are based on FRS3 and are therefore not comparable with previous years
Source: Construction Forecasting and Research Ltd based on company accounts.

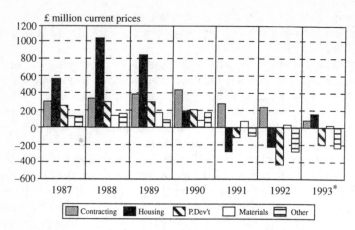

Figure 2.6   Pre-tax profits by activity of 70 of the top 80 UK construction companies 1987–93
*The value shown for 1993 is based on FRS3 and is therefore not comparable with previous years
Source: Construction Forecasting and Research Ltd based on company accounts.

had improved their position by 1993 but seven were making significantly greater (more than 25% greater) losses in 1993.

What was really happening was that large contractors were maintaining contracting turnover by cutting margins and by going down in size of projects into the usual markets of smaller contractors where the higher overheads of the large contractors puts them at a disadvantage. This was a time when the number of large contracts was shrinking faster than the total workload so that, even if they simply maintained market shares, large contractors would have had to go down in size of contract. To increase their market share they needed to go down into even smaller contracts.

Reference

1. Hillebrandt, Patricia M. and Cannon, Jacqueline, *The Modern Construction Firm* (London: Macmillan, 1990).

Part II
The Contractors and their Strategies

3 Financial Considerations

3.1 INTRODUCTION

There have been dramatic changes in the finances of the companies interviewed since the collapse of the boom. These have affected their capital structure, their profits and cash flow. Their responses included stricter financial control, cost cutting and cuts in dividends. The sections below discuss the change from boom to recession, the predicament faced by the companies and their reactions.

Because of over-borrowing, capital requirements became a preoccupation of contractors and this is dealt with first in the next section. This is followed by sections on profits (3.3), on dividends (3.4) and share values (3.5). The important subject of cash flow in various parts of the business is dealt with in Section 3.6. The related subject of bonding and credit is in Section 3.7. Financial control and external influences are considered in Section 3.8 and 3.9 respectively.

In the presentation of data in tables and graphs, where possible all eighteen companies are included. For several, however, information is not published due to their particular company structure.

Table 3.1 below summarises some of the reactions of the companies in the survey to the recession from 1989 to 1993.

This analysis is similar to that undertaken in a major study of British industry by Geroski and Gregg.[1] All actions in the list above are more important in the construction industry than in British industry as a whole because of the far more serious decline in the former from the late 1980s.

3.2 CAPITAL

In the second half of the 1980s there was a boom in lending for all purposes. Banks were trying to persuade companies that it was beneficial to borrow money to invest in the expansion of their businesses. At the same time Stock Exchange analysts were suggesting that any company which was not utilising borrowed money for growth was not taking advantage of the opportunities available to it and was therefore a poor investment

37

Table 3.1   Actions taken in response to recession during the period 1989 to
           1993

Action	Number of firms*
Write-down asset values	11
Disposal of businesses	10
Conversion of debt to equity	1
Substantial rescheduling of debt	2
Rights issues	7
Reduce dividends	12
Reduce number of offices	7
Reduce head office costs	13
Reduce employment costs	13
Total number of firms covered	14

*Some firms have been excluded from this analysis because they are private
companies, have been taken over, recently merged or are owned by foreign
firms.
Source: The interviews.

compared with those companies which were borrowing. As it happened
the construction companies themselves were keen on growth. In interviews carried out in 1986 almost all companies were seeking profitable
growth and in some it was the dominant objective. Thus many were
easily persuaded of the merits of borrowing to finance growth.

It was not only the quest for profits which made growth attractive.
There was a common view that diversification was desirable per se and
this was easier to achieve if the company was growing. In addition
some companies were very anxious to enhance their asset base partly to
permit the easier raising of funds in the future and partly to impress the
Stock Exchange with their strength. As a result many firms over-
borrowed. Indeed, at its peak, bank lending to construction companies
reached a record level and the Bank of England warned that some
restraint was necessary. The number of companies in the survey (for
which data are available) which had over 50% gearing increased from
one to four from 1988 to 1992 and in 1992 one had over 400% gearing.
On the other hand the companies with less than 5% gearing increased
from four to five and four companies remained the same during the
period. The number of firms studied is too small to provide findings

which are statistically significant but the results are not inconsistent with the relationships in the seventy large companies on which data are given in Section 2.2. The optimism of the late 1980s was such that companies regarded their high gearing as a temporary phenomenon which would correct itself as soon as their investments paid off. However, in the process of expansion, the balance of the business, in terms of cash-using and cash-generating operations, had been disturbed. Moreover not enough attention was directed to consideration of future balance sheets. This is partly because, in reasonably prosperous times, contractors are concerned with turnover and profitability and, because of positive cash flow, they do not need to consider capital requirements in any detail. The effect of the recession on their capital intensive businesses was much quicker than on contracting.

Companies had invested in a variety of businesses but mainly in property which they were constructing, in land for housing and by purchasing companies in the UK or abroad which seemed to offer attractive opportunities for diversification. The collapse in both the property and housing markets took them by surprise. Construction companies were left with offices, shops and other properties which could neither be sold nor let and with land for housing for which the demand had evaporated. In this situation there was no likelihood of paying off loans and reducing gearing as would have been expected in the normal course of business operations. A few companies realised their predicament earlier than others and sold, albeit at a loss. Others waited until there were no buyers to be had at any price and had to retain these white elephants.

They may well have feared tough action by the banks but, as it happened, the banks were concerned with trying to keep open the possibility of eventually retrieving existing loans. The banks therefore helped companies to survive. This policy has maintained surplus capacity in the industry thus endangering the short-term prospects for a return to a normal level of profits and the longer term viability of even the more efficient companies. Whether or not the banks will have benefitted by this policy in the long run depends on whether the firms they have supported survive which in turn depends largely on the future workload of the industry and the management of the firms concerned.

At the same time the balance sheet values of property and land of previous years had become totally unrealistic. Assets had to be written down. Partly as a result of this, gearing increased from already high levels to, in some cases, unprecedented and disastrous levels. Where contractors shared in the financing of projects for which bank support might not be available, they had set up joint companies with property developers in which each held 50% of the equity. This enabled them to avoid showing those investments in their balance sheets. Thus, investment in property by construction companies was even greater than was known by the outside world. When the bubble burst the losses were correspondingly high. When the property companies folded, the construction companies were further exposed to possible failure. Some companies postponed the painful process of writing down assets in the hope of an upturn. In general, however, those that wrote down their assets earlier were able to turn their attention to constructive policies of rebuilding their balance sheets sooner and benefitted as a result. Moreover those which anticipated a long recession earlier were better able to cope with the financial problems which followed.

An indication of the extent of writing down of assets is shown by the size of 'exceptional items' in balance sheets. In the companies studied they were small or nil in 1989 and 1990 but in 1991 and 1992 they increased substantially. They decreased again in 1993. Table 3.2 shows the changes from 1992 to 1993 only, because changes in accounting standards in the past two years prevent comparisons with earlier years. Not all the companies in the survey are included because the ownership structure of some companies is such that the data are not available.

Another reason for the large increase in exceptional items was the provision for redundancy costs which were very substantial as companies slashed management, often by around a third.

As explained above high gearing was now another serious problem facing companies. It was essential to reduce high gearing because:

- it was regarded by the stock market as putting companies at risk and led to sharp falls in share values;
- it implied very high interest costs;
- it gave banks control over expenditure and could allow them to become involved in the running of the company and, if they so decided, to foreclose;
- it made it impossible for companies to participate in providing finance for projects;
- it made it difficult to convince potential clients that the company was strong enough to complete a contract;
- it made it difficult to obtain bonds.

Table 3.2   Exceptional items in balance sheets   (£000s)

Company	1992	Restated 1992	1993
Balfour Beatty Ltd	−8 000	−8 000	0
Boot (Henry) & Sons plc	0	0	0
Bovis Construction Ltd	199	199	0
Costain Group plc	−133 300	−188 600	−68 500
Galliford plc	−703	−703	−846
Higgs & Hill plc	−11 981	−12 345	0
Kier Group plc			
Laing (John) plc	−21 400	−21 400	−2 700
Lovell (YJ) Holdings plc	−14 422	−21 616	−26 703
Miller Group Ltd	−4 675	−4 675	−6 625
Mowlem (John) & Co plc	−20 200	−38 500	−99
Tarmac plc	−372 000	−372 000	−96 500
Taylor Woodrow plc	−66 400	−66 400	−8 300
Try Group plc	−800	−3 020	−1 738
Willmot Dixon Ltd	28	28	−806
Wilson (Connolly) Hldgs plc	−5 488	−5 488	0
Wimpey (George) plc	−113 800	−113 000	−3 100
Total	**−772 942**	**−855 520**	**−215 917**

Source: Construction Forecasting Research Ltd based on company accounts.

There are two main ways of reducing gearing: the sale of assets to pay off loans or raising capital.

Companies sold assets in order to pay back some of their loans or even to pay the interest on loans. Unfortunately, as the assets they most wanted to sell had little value, they were forced to sell businesses which were profitable and which, in other circumstances, they would have wished to retain. The result was that the balance between various parts of the company did not necessarily change in the way which was most beneficial to its future health. Moreover any business which was thought soon to require a major injection of capital was a prime target for a sale. Disposal of cash consuming businesses became a major objective of some companies.

Types of businesses disposed of in the period to the end of 1993 included plant hire, land restoration, environmental control, waste treatment, housebuilding, joinery, coal mining, property, leisure and product manufacture. It was not always easy to sell some of those businesses which were not in good shape, unless they were offered at an attractively low price. In the case of a business in good fettle there was a choice of either selling to a trade buyer or arranging a management buy-out or floating it on the market. Some senior executives of one contractor thought that it would be possible to get a successful flotation for a major subsidiary but the board wanted certainty and there were several interested buyers. It eventually played safe and sold to a trade buyer.

The main fixed assets of contracting businesses are plant and equipment, and buildings. Some companies which had plant hire businesses, both for their own use and to hire out, have sold them and now hire what they need. Others still prefer to keep their own key plant even if it is not very profitable. One company, which owned a group plant supplier, tightly controlled any external hire as it was very wary of the plant hire industry. Another contractor had a thriving plant hire business and made a good profit, but this was partly because it also hired-out prefabricated buildings, for example to schools and hospitals, and the business did not suffer the same cycles as contracting.

Contractors closed a number of regional offices and cut back on head office space. Where the offices were rented and the firms were able to terminate the buildings or sub-let the lease there was a clear gain in cost reduction. Where they are owned, in the present environment, some space is proving difficult to sell or let but at least running costs have been reduced through 'mothballing' of whole buildings.

Companies not only sold assets to reduce gearing but also tried to renegotiate the remaining loans and raised capital for the same purpose. This included reducing the number of lenders and negotiating with the greater freedom of action thus obtained, provided gearing was not too high. One company persuaded the banks to which it owed large sums to convert the loans into equity and hence substantially reduced gearing. The effect of the restrictions placed by banks on companies included eliminating options for business development, and it stopped them from taking advantage of opportunities for investment in new ventures. The sheer number of companies in difficulties prevented the banks from exercising the tight control over management that they would otherwise have imposed.

Rights issues, an alternative way to reduce gearing, was adopted by a number of companies. Of the companies interviewed eight out of the fourteen for which it was relevant have had rights issues or raised equity since the beginning of 1990s.

The best time to go to the market to raise capital is when a company appears in reasonable shape and therefore does not urgently need funds. Of the rights issues above two companies were clearly in this situation. The rights issues gave them a healthier balance sheet and headroom to expand in the future. Most companies, however, were in more urgent need of finance. On the surface it appears puzzling that shareholders were willing to invest more money in companies which were clearly in some difficulty. However institutions and other investors with a substantial stake in a company prefer to put in funds rather than risk the loss of their total investment. Banks also do not want to lose the money they have lent and encourage rights issues for the same reasons as being willing to lend. The underwriters know the consequence of not supporting an issue though their rates of commission for doing so rise as the risks of being left with unsold shares increases. Moreover they usually agree with institutions before the launch of the issue for them to take up a part of the issue, and this is often arranged at a discount which, in exceptional circumstances, can be 20–30%. Lastly the workings of the financial institutions ensure that there is a flow of money to be invested. Institutions can hold-off for a while but eventually they need to invest their accumulating funds. Provided a rights issue is timed so that it does not coincide with too many other cash calls, the institutions are generally willing to invest. The situation in the UK stock market relative to the rest of the world also has to be considered. When for example Wall Street is down, US funds look for investments elsewhere and, as one finance director commented, 'investors are like lemmings, if you convince a few the rest will follow'.

The doleful situation with respect to the balance sheets affected most of the publicly quoted companies interviewed but in some the damage was limited because they were not so heavily involved in the purchase of assets, of property, of land for housing or of other companies. In particular one company had been in very serious difficulties in the first half of the 1980s and when these difficulties were overcome, while boom conditions obtained, it remained very cautious and conservative in its policies. Due to its caution that company is in a better position now than many other companies. In general family controlled companies have been more circumspect than others and appear to have fared better during the last few difficult years.

It is undoubtedly true that the troubles of the construction companies were as much a result of their behaviour in the boom as in the recession itself. Many of these difficulties could have been avoided if they had been less caught up in the euphoria of the boom. Similarly it is agreed that companies could have anticipated the collapse in the property and housing markets. It had been clear for some time before the collapse in the property market that an oversupply of offices was inevitable but by the time this was realised by construction companies they had invested too much in their schemes to be able to withdraw. In any case the boom conditions seemed to create an unwillingness to face the fact that it would end. When the Chancellor of the Exchequer announced in the 1988 Spring Budget the cessation of more than one mortgage tax relief for any one property in the following August, the industry should have realised that this would create a boom and then a fall in the housing market as a whole. However, few realised just how dramatically housing transactions would fall. The NEDO Forecast for private housing in June 1988[2] did not mention the budget. It was not until December 1988[3] that it was realised that first time buyers would have brought forward their purchases to the summer 1988 with a resulting fall in demand in 1989. In any case profits from housing were running so high that it would have taken a brave board to recommend stopping all land purchases.

There is another factor relating to the mechanism by which many companies buy land which maintains the momentum. Some land is bought with planning permission at a given price. This is a simple and relatively speedy transaction and it is possible quickly to stop such purchases. Much land, however, is bought without planning permission at a percentage of the current price (depending on how long it is expected it will take to obtain the permission) and payment is made when planning permission is obtained. These transactions cannot be stopped and, until the forward contracts have run out, land continues to be bought.

Overall the capital re-arrangements, though difficult and painful, were probably less damaging to the firm internally than some of the cost cutting that also had to take place. Some firms commented that the former were largely 'on paper' with consequences for growth, whilst with the latter jobs were at stake.

Table 3.3   Turnover and pre-tax profits/losses of companies in survey
(£million)

Company	1989 Turnover	Profit	1992 Turnover	Profit	1993 Turnover	Profit
Balfour Beatty Ltd	1 575.0	48.0	1 881.0	39.9	1831.0	51.6
Boot (Henry) & Sons plc	136.1	5.4	129.4	7.1	164.6	7.6
Bovis Construction Ltd	711.1	32.0	460.1	9.6	366.1	12.9
Costain Group plc	1 327.9	22.7	1 272.9	–204.6	1 104.7	68.7
Galliford plc	197.3	9.8	213.2	3.0	217.2	0.4
Higgs & Hill plc	419.0	23.7	296.0	–22.0	262.0	1.2
Kier Group plc			545.4	5.5	512.2	5.6
Laing (John) plc	1 363.2	57.5	1 269.5	11.6	1 263.9	18.3
Lovell (YJ) Holdings plc	384.8	23.8	274.8	–27.0	221.3	–59.3
Miller Group Ltd	255.7	21.5	257.6	–2.1	357.6	–11.9
Mowlem (John) & Co plc	1 305.0	30.4	1 237.0	–38.5	1 269.0	–124.2
Tarmac plc	3 409.2	377.0	2 934.9	–350.3	2 669.2	–43.1
Taylor Woodrow plc	1 285.4	79.3	1 245.2	–94.5	1 149.7	30.2
Try Group plc	95.6	4.3	117.9	–0.7	124.2	–2.2
Willmot Dixon Ltd	87.6	1.3	152.3	1.1	191.1	–1.4
Wilson (Connolly) Hldgs plc	193.0	54.0	201.0	17.0	274.0	28.0
Wimpey (George) plc	2 065.0	123.8	1 639.2	–111.6	1 587.4	25.5
Total	**14 810.9**	**914.5**	**14 127.4**	**–756.5**	**13 565.2**	**7.9**

Note: Profits have been restated under FRS3.
The 1993 figures for Kier Group are for the period 21 April 1992 to 30
June 1993
Source: Construction Forecasting and Research Ltd based on company
accounts.

By the end of 1993 the various measures adopted by companies had
been successful in producing more satisfactory balance sheets with
gearing down to acceptable levels. However by 1994, because of
losses, the gearing of some firms started to rise again because they
could not fund capital spending internally, for example for new land in
housing. The crisis in capital structure was therefore dealt with to a

large extent but the preoccupation has now shifted to dealing with very low levels of profitability.

3.3   PROFITS

It was not only in terms of the balance sheet that companies suffered. Profits fell in all types of businesses: in property because it could not be let nor sold profitably - indeed the cost of holding assets was greater than the profit generated; in housing, because houses could not be sold. In contracting profits shrank because the shortage of work had led to low tender prices and tiny or negative margins. The main reason for low bids has been the need to maintain cash flow at a satisfactory level. Another reason was to retain high calibre management teams.

Overall profits of the companies in the survey of some £900 million were transformed by 1992 into a loss of £750 million. In 1993 there was a small profit of £8 million. Table 3.3 below compares turnover and profits or losses in the main types of business in the companies visited at the peak year for profits of 1989 and the trough of 1992.

The largest losses were made in housing followed by property and contracting. Figure 3.1 shows profits or losses by types of work for the companies in the study for the years 1987 to 1993.

Tender prices were very low throughout the early 1990s though they rose for the first time in the fourth quarter of 1993. According to the analysis undertaken by Davis Langdon and Everest tender prices fell by 33% percent from the start of their fall in the fourth quarter of 1989 to the apparent end of the fall in the third quarter of 1993. Some contractors tendered so low that they did not cover overheads. A few were said to have tendered below site costs though those interviewed denied that they did so.

In early 1994 this may have been a reasonable strategy if it was thought that the recession was nearly over as those contracts with negative margins were still making a positive cash contribution. Moreover if the trend of materials and labour prices was still downwards the companies might be able to retrieve some profit in the final outcome. However for companies which face further falls in turnover and cash flow, the outlook remains dire. The only salvation would be further borrowing from the

£ million current prices

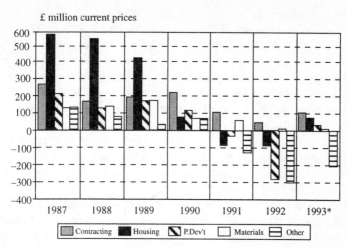

Figure 3.1 Pre-tax profits by activity of 17 companies in the survey 1989–93
*The 1993 analysis is based on FRS3 and is therefore not directly comparable
with previous years
Source: Construction Forecasting and Research Ltd based on company accounts.

banks. In late 1993 banks seemed reluctant to refuse loans, at least to
some large companies, because they already had so much at stake in them.

Tendering below site cost is rarely justified. One contractor,
however, explained that this can happen because the actual costs are
higher than expected, a common occurrence on a proportion of contracts. More dangerously estimators who are anxious to keep their jobs
can be tempted to put in low cost estimates to improve the chances of
winning a contract. It can be difficult for board members to gauge
whether estimators are 'sharpening their pencils' too much. This situation is similar to that discovered by a firm undertaking a review of its
tendering policy in a period of relatively stable demand. It was found
that if the firm put in a higher mark-up across the board it would
receive fewer contracts but overall would make more money. As a
result the company resolved to follow this policy. However, the estimating department was aware of this policy and reduced cost estimates
so that tender prices actually fell rather than rose!

One contractor observed that overheads for construction in his company were about $4\frac{1}{2}\%$. However, in the market of late 1993 the level of mark-up plus interest from positive cash flow was less than $4\frac{1}{2}\%$. Other contractors gave similar examples – overheads 4%, mark up 2% plus less than 1% for interest on cash flow. It was also noted that because of higher risks and because demand had not fallen as much in civil engineering as in building, margins in civil engineering were higher than in building. In building competition was between diverse companies, some of which were prepared to bid unrealistically low prices. One contractor summed up the problem thus: 'If you don't win work you go out of business; if you win work at a loss you also go out of business but it takes longer'.

Risk is extremely important in determining whether mark-up levels are adequate. Risks are for example, that the client pays late or not at all; that the job is underpriced and that the job is more complex than anticipated. Risk has to be balanced against the commercial advantages of the job, for example, the size of the gap in order books for that type of work. The strategy of one company was to limit the size of jobs undertaken to the level at which the failure of one project would not endanger the company. They wanted to have a 'low risk profile in what is a high risk business'.

Companies in the recession, in order to obtain turnover, bid for more as well as smaller projects. In doing so the large contractors eroded the market of the medium sized contractors.

Companies are aware of the great dangers to profit as the industry comes out of recession. Contracts may be easier to obtain and prices may improve but the likelihood is that the costs of materials, plant and labour will rise sharply as workload grows. Indeed, there was evidence of this even in late 1993. Bricklayers were identified as the first trade likely to increase in price in the short-term. Although companies express a preference for short-term contracts in order to limit cost escalation, in practice they are driven to take long-term contracts on a fixed price basis by the need to get work. In spite of their awareness of the potential problems, there is thus a danger that low or negative profits will in future come from rising costs whereas in the past they have come from low prices. It is very difficult to buy forward because suppliers will not accept such deals and many quantities are too small. The situation is made worse where firms have been locked into long-term fixed price contracts on which fluctuation clauses have been rare and because clients are resistant to such clauses even for large contracts. The importance of claims has changed little overall although it is possible that contractors are willing to settle at rather lower levels to get the money in quickly. However in road construction final account figures are said to run up to as much as 40% above tender prices.

Return on capital employed can be infinite in contracting and therefore it is not a relevant measure of performance. For housing, however, return on capital employed after interest is very important. The advantage of housing is that if houses are not selling a firm can stop building. It can also go on to complete and sell them at a lower price than budgeted. There is an exit route. Thus, the comparison between various businesses must be based on the balance between the total profit for each of them compared with their individual risks.

3.4 DIVIDENDS

The recessionary situation and low profits would suggest that it was reasonable for firms to cut dividends sharply in order to reduce the money outflow, to be realistic in relation to the health of the company and to show employees that they were not the only ones to suffer in a recession. However, dividends in construction have fallen remarkably little. Even when companies were making considerable losses they still kept dividends up or even increased them. Figure 3.2 shows how dividends have changed from 1989 to 1993; changes in profits are also shown for comparison.

There was a difference of opinion about dividend policy even within the companies interviewed. Whilst several executives were in favour of drastic cuts, in fact other factors arguing for minimal cuts were seen to be very persuasive. One factor was for firms to keep faith with investors relying on the dividend income and this was particularly so for family firms. Another pointed out that the determining factor was to pay the same rate of return as other companies within the sector; that there was very little choice for the individual company and that dividend levels were also related to the share price. Above all it was seen to be necessary to satisfy the Stock Exchange, the analysts and the main investors that the dividend policy was appropriate. A reasonably high level of dividend was also seen to help ensure success for rights issues – a particular feature of this recession (see Section 3.2 on capital). One

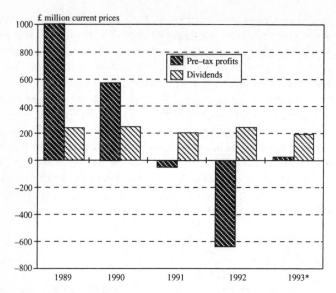

Figure 3.2   Pre-tax profits/losses and dividends of 17 companies in the survey
1989–93
*The value shown for 1993 has been reported under FRS3
The profits prior to 1993 are those declared during each period
(i.e. on which dividends were based).
Source: Construction Forecasting and Research Ltd based on company accounts.

company which had seen a steady rise in profits aimed to increase its
dividend cautiously but more or less in line with profits. However, if
there was no profit it would still usually pay some dividend.

3.5   SHARE VALUES

Share values of construction companies rose to a peak in autumn 1987
and then plummeted before recovering in mid 1988 to a high level in
early 1989. They fell from mid 1989 to late 1992. Since then they have
risen substantially. Figure 3.3 shows these trends for 1986 to spring 1994
and also shows the relationship of the building and construction share
prices to the FTSE 100 index. Relative to the FTSE 100 index building
and construction shares did better during the early years of the boom but
fell by nearly 70% compared to the FTSE 100 index during the recession.
    Publicly quoted companies must be careful that their share values
are not too low for fear of takeovers and even more so when a predator

51

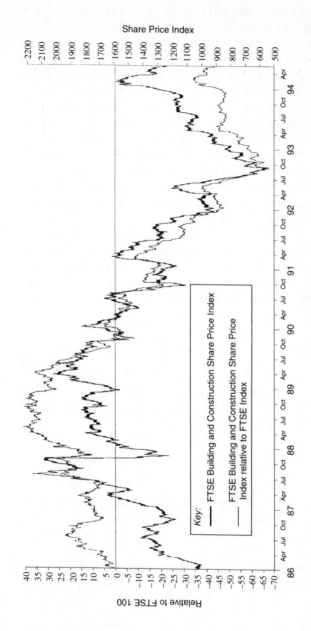

Figure 3.3 FTSE Building and Construction UK Share Prices 1987–94
Source: Extel Financial.

is lurking, waiting for the moment to buy. A low share price and a poor balance sheet means that a firm cannot afford to take actions which would worsen the balance sheet further in the short-term. For example, if a good long-term opportunity arises which it would be advantageous to pursue but will show a short-term loss then it cannot be pursued. An example is Trafalgar House stalking Costain in the period 1987–89. Costain could have sold its stake in the Spitalfields development but this would have meant a write-off of £4 million. It did not dare to do this for fear of market reaction. Similarly it could have sold some housing land in 1988 at a loss but for the same reason it held on. Both these sales would have been beneficial to the long-term health of the company were it not for the expected market reaction in the short-term.

The vulnerability to takeover is even greater when the balance sheet is sound but the share price low because the value of the assets is higher than the market value of the company. Most companies have share market valuations which are about the same as their asset values but recently they have sometimes been less. One company's share value, however, is about twice its asset value. This gives it great strength and reflects the market assessment of its potential.

3.6   CASH FLOW

In the short run cash flow is at least as important as profit. The cash flow problems faced by companies began later than problems of capital largely because the property and housing markets collapsed before construction turnover declined.

3.6.1   Contracting

For traditional and some management contracting cash flow is positive, that is, the companies receive cash on a contract before they have to pay it out. This is because:

● they pay subcontractors at the end of the month for work for which they have themselves already been paid, and some delay such payments;

- they obtain credit from builders' merchants longer than the one month in which they get paid for work done;
- when they price the bill of quantities they may weight the prices of items at the beginning of the contract more heavily than those at the end. This front-end-loading effectively secures a form of pre-payment for work.

In general cash flow is better on fast jobs than slow ones and better on large than small. Over the recession contract periods have reduced, thus improving cash flow and lowering overheads but the average size of contracts has fallen. Design and build contracts which are increasing in importance (See Chapter 5) produce a satisfactory cash flow but management contracts do not. Inevitably there is no easy remedy for contractors with little working capital for a falling cash flow except to delay their payments to others. The principal sufferers are the subcontractors.

Cash flow is generally favourable when turnover is rising and it falls when turnover falls but not necessarily at a comparable rate. It fluctuates monthly because money flows out until the end of the month and then, when the interim certificates are honoured, it flows in again. It is also seasonal; the peaks and troughs depending on the type of work undertaken. For example some architects place some work in the spring so that turnover in the second half of the year is usually higher than in the first half. Also autumn weather is often good. Although the last quarter can be bad for cash flow largely because of the Christmas period the payment of government contracts in the first quarter tends to raise cash flow again because money allocated has to be spent by the end of the financial year. For large contractors cash flow can be squeezed by late payments from clients including property developers and public clients.

Recently, it has been reported that large repeat and corporate clients have become concerned about the payments to contractors which generate a positive cash flow while the client's aim is to keep this negative. They are increasingly scrutinizing bids for front-end loading and are attempting to minimize stage payments. Some contractors reported that, they had failed to win contracts, despite being the lowest bidder, when front-end loading was deemed too high. A few companies expressed the view that payment structures for contracts are likely to change over the next few years in line with clients tougher control over interim payments, to the detriment of contractors. The inability to earn interest on positive cash balances would seriously undermine the present logic applied to the pricing of projects.

Positive cash flow enables companies to earn interest on cash balances or to reduce their overdrafts. During the recession the income from cash flow fell both because cash flow was reduced and because of the drop in interest rates. It may still be the case that the return on positive cash flow remains an important source of profit to contractors at a time when profits have fallen so far. A few companies stressed the need to appreciate that positive cash flow was the client's money paid in advance and, therefore, not the contractor's own. It was not free for use except on a temporary basis. Contractors who invested this cash in semi-permanent assets such as land and then found their cash flow falling faced serious difficulties.

There was no trace of an understanding of the dangers of relying on cash flow to finance long-term investments in the earlier study undertaken in 1986. Indeed the preoccupation then was in finding good capital-intensive long-term investments for utilising the positive cash flow which was regarded as secure. With hindsight this led to the misuse of clients' funds and in itself generated cash problems.

3.6.2   Housing

In the past one of the reasons for construction firms engaging in building houses was that it was a good and profitable use for the cash generated by contracting. With the fall in cash flow during the recession, attitudes have changed. Construction companies now view housing development as a more self-contained operation with the cash flow remaining negative until after completion because of the early outgoings on land, and services for the site. Construction is now carried out by subcontractors. One company arranges for its subcontractors to construct houses as and when required. They are paid on a monthly certificate basis. The contract is fixed price so it is up to the subcontractor when tendering to assess how long it is likely to be before all houses are built, which will depend on demand. He also has to estimate the likely rise in costs over that period. The developer said, however, that if there were major cost rises the company would come to some arrangement with the subcontractor for an upward revision in spite of the contractual conditions, especially as a period of rising costs is usually also one of rising house prices.

The ways to keep negative cash flow as low as possible in housebuilding were variously described as:

- to have a minimum amount of stocks of land;
- to have sites which are not too large and therefore on which houses are constructed and sold fairly quickly;
- to build each house as required and as quickly as possible;
- to take deposits on house sales.

There were differing views about the cash requirement for speculative housing. There is little doubt that over the last few years negative cash flow in housebuilding has been reduced. At one extreme a few contractors claimed that the housing cash flow could be substantially reduced by buying land only when required and if possible on deferred payment terms and by cutting back on other outgoings. In this way the cash required for housing becomes low compared with traditional approaches. One contractor changed from turning over capital in housing from once a year to twice a year. As a result the value of work in progress on site has been halved. However, at the other extreme it was pointed out that at least a two year land bank was necessary as each site has to last two years. It takes about 12 months from purchase of a site to first conveyance and then the other houses would be sold in the following year. In the USA the situation is different, it is possible to buy or at least pay for land as it is used.

In 1993 land banks ranged from 1.5 years supply to around 4 years with contractors' housing divisions generally at the lower end of the range. In 1992 the land banks were larger, with a range of 2 to 5 years. Incidentally, the habit in the industry of measuring the land bank by the number of years supply has the consequence that if the rate of construction slows the same stock of land measured in these terms actually increases.

3.6.3 Property

Property developers fall into two distinctive groups: traders whose sole aim is to conceive a project, undertake the development and sell at a profit, and investors/developers who undertake projects in the same way but with the aim of adding to their portfolios. A few of the major contractors also operate as both traders and investors in their own right. During the second half of the 1980s, several contractors chose to link with traders in joint ventures in a manner described as off-balance sheet financing. Under the arrangement, both parties had equal shares in a particular project which permitted short-term finance to be kept off both companies' balance sheets and thus concealed the total extent of developers' reliance on short-term borrowings to finance projects under construction.

Developers have choices in the sale or disposal of projects, which are influenced by the current and expected state of the property market, by their own financial situation and ease of borrowing, by their assessment of the various risks associated with the project etc. If traders assess demand to be near its peak, they will attempt to pre-fund, with investors putting up the necessary funds to cover all costs of the project, including acquisition of land and all incidentals. Another alternative is forward commitment whereby the investor undertakes to purchase on completion at a price, fixed at the time the contract is signed, either before or during construction. The third is to seek a buyer at completion.

When the commercial property market collapsed, contractors involved in property development suffered the same fate as developers. Not all those in the survey were seriously involved in it and for those which kept out of it, cash flow problems were obviously less acute.

For those contractors which either on their own or jointly with developers either presold developments or obtained investors' funding, there were no cash flow problems arising from this activity. For those who intended to retain developments in their portfolio, the main problems were financing beyond the short-term and ability to let. Even where leases could be arranged, the lower rents obtained would generate a cash flow profile well below that used in the income estimates which had justified construction.

3.6.4 Mining and minerals

There are three factors to be considered: the cost of purchasing the mine and the mining rights; the cost of plant to extract the mineral, and the operating costs. There are differences in the way in which companies assess these costs in cash flow terms.

Whether the cash flow from mining and mineral extraction is regarded as positive or negative depends first of all on whether the initial purchase is regarded as an outflow or not. Because it is a long-term investment some companies consider it is reasonable to assume it is not an outflow and thus some contractors say that there is a positive cash flow because the value of the sales of the mineral normally exceed substantially the marginal costs of production including the marginal cost of plant. Although it lasts a long time plant is very expensive so in a recession purchase of new plant is postponed. However, perhaps because of the low capital investment and high cash flow traditions of contracting some firms do regard minerals as a cash outflow business.

3.7   BONDING AND CREDIT

In recent years the use of bonds has increased considerably, especially for large contracts. Strictly speaking if the contractor is in good financial health and has a sound reputation, a bond should be unnecessary but, if it is required, there should be no difficulty in the contractor obtaining one. If the contractor is not sound, in normal circumstances the client would not include him in the tender list. If that contractor is on the tender list the necessary bond will be difficult to obtain and expensive. However because so many contractors have gone through a difficult period bonds have now become commonplace. Conversely contractors are sometimes now requiring bonds from clients to protect themselves from non-payment.

The type of bond normally used in the UK is the 'surety bond'. The bond is for 10% of the contract sum and the contractor takes out an insurance bond to this value from Lloyds or from a bank or some specialist financial institution. In the event that the contractor does not fulfil the contract conditions or goes bankrupt, then the bond is called in and the client with this insurance money should be able to complete the work. However there is room for argument as to how much of the bond sum is in fact due to the client. There can be disputes, for example on the value of work already completed and cost of variations and so forth. Because of arguments over surety bonds some clients have required 'on-demand' bonds. The procedure with these is that the client receives the money and argues later about whether it is due. This system is open to abuse because clients have called in bonds when it was not appropriate to do so. Traditionally banks had made a modest charge for bonds but on-demand bonds are now treated as equivalent to an overdraft and their cost is high. On-demand bonds are commonly used overseas and London Underground is reported to be requiring them but their use in the UK is still small.

A recent case in the court of appeal: *Trafalgar House Construction (Regions) Limited v. General Surety and Guarantee Co Limited* (1994) 66 BLR 42 ruled that, if the client claims an amount on a surety bond in good faith then the money should be paid. This may overcome some of the arguments over surety bonds which has brought them into disrepute. The case is subject to appeal.

For large projects, because they have a low capital base, UK contractors are at a disadvantage compared with French and German contractors which have much higher capital assets and from which the banks have no problems in accommodating requests for credit. For large projects UK companies are often linked to European ones. Indeed, in one or two large joint-venture projects which have been executed or are planned, one of the reasons for a UK firm having a foreign partner is the capital structure of the latter. There are some international regulations which should assist credit arrangements, notably the Basle Convergence Agreement which unifies them for all countries.

3.8   FINANCIAL CONTROL WITHIN COMPANIES

In 1989, as detailed earlier, problems were looming for many companies, with housing businesses consuming cash too quickly and escalating funding requirements of the property businesses. At the same time additional businesses were being bought, often without adequate consideration and at too high a price.

A company with reasonable financial control should have been able to estimate that it would not be able to finance all its commitments, even without an allowance for a collapse in asset values which it was acknowledged was not anticipated until much too late. As a result of the failure to foresee what happened, companies have since strengthened financial control by the following methods:

- tighter cost control;
- stricter cash flow monitoring;

● better budget planning and use of funds.

Costs have been reduced or controlled, including by:

● staff redundancies;
● reorganisation of divisions and regional offices to lower overheads; in some cases service functions have been transferred to head office;
● slimming of head office; in some cases by making regional offices or divisions responsible for more service functions; in one case this involved closure of the head office of a major but relatively separate part of the business;
● control over capital expenditure on new acquisitions, on land for housing and on plant and machinery;
● salary freezes or even salary cuts and no bonuses;
● reduction in number and size of company cars;
● less training;
● reduction of frequency of formal compilation and reporting of accounting information to save accounting staff and meeting times made possible by improved computer access to routine data.

Lastly, the planning of budgets has generally been improved and their monitoring greatly tightened. Most companies have a financial budget for one year to eighteen months ahead but they appear to have gone into greater detail than in 1986 – the time of the previous study.

3.9   EXTERNAL INFLUENCES

Banks, Stock Exchange analysts, institutional shareholders and major clients and competitors all have some bearing on companies' financial behaviour and hence affect the industry as a whole.

In a recessionary period, when debts to banks are high, the influence of the banks is very strong. A company which is at risk may be asked by its bankers to manage its business differently, to produce more frequent financial data and a revised corporate plan, or to recruit a particular board member. One company with substantial debts to banks said that they had been restricted in considering various options for growth and development. However, the banks influence has also been considerable in maintaining some companies in business. They have refrained from calling in loans from companies which could not service them or repay them and have not refused further loans to large companies which would otherwise have had to call in the receivers. The reason is that the banks had so much invested in these companies that they hoped to salvage their investment by an additional injection of funds. Banks seem to have been less willing to support smaller companies as reflected in campaigns such as those of the Chartered Institute of Building, which aimed to achieve a more sympathetic response by banks to the difficulties of small builders.

The consequence of the banks' support for the larger companies is that the capacity of the industry at the upper levels has not reduced sufficiently. If in the future demand does not rise to the levels of the height of the boom in 1989, and many companies think it will not, then the capacity of the industry needs in some way to be reduced. It is difficult to see how this will happen (see Section 9.1 for a further discussion of this matter).

Another influential group is Stock Exchange analysts. Some contractors resented the power and influence of relatively young inexperienced analysts. A report of an analyst can change the share price of a company overnight and hence its ability to raise money, or the likelihood of being taken over. Some analysts are regarded as unscrupulous in putting their own interpretation on statements by board members and in trying to influence investors' behaviour.

The problem with the Stock Exchange is that its judgements are essentially short-term. The stock market demands profits to be maintained at least in line with its expectations. This short-termism makes engaging in risky ventures and investing in innovations with a long-term pay-back dangerous. Accounting rules preclude holding back reserves and the whole position of the company has to be very open. It is understood that the way the German system works permits a longer term view to be taken by companies especially when they are linked to German banks. In the UK some companies have turned down some business options because of the short-term effects on their Stock Exchange rating, even though the outcome would have been in their long-term interests. One company should have sold some of its property at a loss but could not do so because it could not afford to show a loss in its balance sheet. A year or so later a buyer could not be found for the asset. Now the asset is of little value or use to the firm. It must be concluded that the power of the stock market together with its short-termism is damaging to the industry. This issue is amply illustrated in a recent survey by Coopers & Lybrand[4] which showed that four out of five managers in medium sized firms drawn from across all industries named short-termism in the city as the biggest single cause of the UK's post-war decline. Institutional shareholders are very influential and companies must ensure their support in some major decisions. Their interests are longer term than those of the Stock Exchange and their influence is, on the whole, benign.

Lastly other companies, including competitors, influence the way construction companies operate, particularly when a possibility of a takeover or merger exists. Moreover major clients may refrain from placing orders with a company which they consider to be at risk and therefore they too have to be convinced of its soundness.

In support of this view was one private company, which made the point that one of the good aspects of being private was that they did not have to worry about share price movements. They said it was valuable 'not having to say what they might not want to say, but at the same time it kept pressures off the group which then led to a need for it to create its own pressures to keep people on their toes'! It may also be tempting for some private companies to err on the cautious side, to lack ambition and thus to fail to capitalize on opportunities.

References

1. Geroski, P.A. and Gregg, P., 'Coping with the Recession', *National Institute Economic Review*, November 1993, pp. 64–75.
2. Joint Forecasting Committee for the Construction Industries, *Construction Forecasts 1988–1989–1990* (London: NEDO, June 1988).
3. Joint Forecasting Committee for the Construction Industries, *Construction Forecasts 1988–1989–1990* (London: NEDO, December 1988).
4. Coopers & Lybrand, *The Middle Market Survey* (London: Coopers & Lybrand, 1994).

4 Markets and Marketing

4.1 INTRODUCTION

This chapter highlights the reduction in the scope of the domestic construction business (Section 4.2). It deals with the main markets in which construction firms operate, namely contracting (4.3), housing (4.4), property (4.5), mining and minerals (4.6), and international businesses (4.7). Under the contracting heading the response of contractors to falling workload and profits is briefly examined. A fuller study of contracting markets is undertaken in Chapter 5.

Lastly the chapter includes a consideration of the way in which contractors market their services starting with the place of markets and marketing in the corporate plan, the structure of their marketing organisations and an assessment of the status of marketing strategy (4.8).

4.2 RETREAT TO CORE BUSINESSES

The 1980s was a period when turnover of construction firms was growing and they were diversifying into construction-related businesses and in some cases into businesses with little connection with construction. The earlier study identified five reasons for diversification: to increase profitable growth; to seek different activities in which this might be achieved; to increase efficiency by controlling supplies or to link activities to achieve a greater synergy; to make good use of positive cash flow and to increase fixed assets; to avoid dependence on the cyclical nature of construction and particular clients and markets.

This diversification resulted in new or greater investment principally in property, housing, building materials, coal and other mining, plant, mechanical and electrical engineering, and builders merchants. Companies also engaged in a miscellaneous range of activities including time-share accommodation, health care, airports and waste disposal as well as some traditional construction businesses in some foreign markets. In the early 1990s these longer term diversification strategies were abandoned for the sake of immediate survival. Thus many of these businesses were disposed of during the recession. The disposals fell into two main categories: those which were felt to be no longer part of the core operations and those which were profitable but were sold to reduce gearing. However, some firms still have businesses which they cannot sell.

Once the crisis was over firms were able to reconsider their strategies and to start to rebuild their strength in their core businesses. Table 4.1 below shows the businesses which the contractors themselves describe as core.

Apart from one company, which is a housing specialist, contracting is the key business and the other 'core' businesses are of lesser importance.

It is interesting that the drive for diversification by construction firms in the 1980s and the subsequent retreat in the 1990s came around ten years later than the corresponding moves in larger firms in UK industry as a whole. The survey undertaken by Geroski and Gregg[1] found that 'Firms who in the 1960s and 1970s diversified their activities in many directions began, in the 1980s, to refocus their activities onto their core businesses' (p. 9).

Several contractors said that they were not comfortable with some of the businesses they had acquired in the 1980s which had little to do with their major activities and for which they did not have the necessary expertise. When asked about future diversification a contractor

Table 4.1 Core businesses of construction companies

Business		Number of companies
Contracting		10
of which Building	3	
Building and Civil Engineering	6	
Civil and Process Engineering	1	
Contracting and Housing		2
Contracting, Housing and Property		2
Contracting, Housing and Minerals		1
Contracting and Mining or Other		2
Housing		1
Total		18

Source: Interviews.

said 'not in this generation'. Yet, as will be discussed later, diversification has been a theme of the recession, but this has taken a different form (see Chapter 5).

4.3 CONTRACTING

The fall in profits in contracting may be seen from Figure 2.6 for large firms generally and from Figure 3.1 for companies in the survey. The reasons include the fall in the volume of work in the industry as a whole (see Figure 1.1) and particularly in large projects which has forced large contractors to go into the market for lower value jobs, normally undertaken by smaller companies, while the number of large firms has decreased only marginally. The large firms are thus competing with many more firms than previously. Nevertheless they have managed actually to increase their turnover in contracting (see Figure 2.4). This increase in turnover has been achieved at the expense of profits.

Tender prices have fallen dramatically with many contractors bidding without making a significant contribution to their overheads and some bidding below site costs. In the early part of the recession they hoped to recover those costs and overheads through lower material and subcontractor costs and, to some extent, through claims and variations. Moreover they would rather take on work at very low or negative margins to maintain cash flow and to retain their management rather than dismiss staff and make high redundancy payments. Some denied that they bid below cost whilst others produced eloquent arguments to explain why apparently negative mark-ups were really positive. Even those who denied bidding at below cost considered that many of their competitors were doing so. Hence they felt that if they did not follow the market down they would lose turnover, staff and their capability to do work and they would eventually go out of business. If they obtained work below cost then cash flow would keep them going for a period, hopefully until an upturn in prices and workload. At the same time as long as they secured work and payment for it, banks were less likely to withdraw support (see Chapter 3).

The number of very large building contracts, which are the preserve of the large firms, are thought to have declined considerably whereas civil engineering contracts have declined less. Through their regional offices the large companies are now competing with relatively small local firms for contracts of, say, £250,000 and much less in some cases where they have a small works departments. Companies are now deliberately shortening their order books because of the danger of escalation of costs. One company which had a number of regional offices had 60% of its turnover in 'small' projects which, it claimed, gave it stability but it also led to a hand to mouth existence since there was no certainty about workload beyond about one year. In another company, at the smaller end of those interviewed, policy had always been to restrict the size of contracts to reduce risk.

Firms have adapted to their changed environment in two main ways. The first is by the extension of existing services and the second by either offering new services or new ways of supplying existing services. These are discussed in detail in Chapter 5.

4.4 HOUSING DEVELOPMENT

The collapse of the housing market in 1989 elicited varying responses, both in terms of timing and scale. Even after the Budget announcement of the abolition of joint mortgage tax relief and with five months warning, the companies did not recognise that recession was likely. They continued to buy land at boom prices throughout the first eight months of 1988. By 1990 a major recession was recognised by most but not all of them.

One of the reasons was that housing divisions of contractors were making good profits. It needed a brave head office management team to persuade a housing division to stop buying land. Many contractors now acknowledge that they 'left the management of the housing divisions too free a hand in land acquisition which was ultimately a disaster for the balance sheet'. One even said 'the boom destroyed rational judgement'. Another described the construction industry as 'a lot of lemmings following each other to disaster'. Some contractors stopped buying land relatively early – late 1988 – but others went on buying land for some time after this.

Some companies followed the market down with successive massive reductions in prices until a new price level was found. A number of housebuilders resorted to non-price incentives to sell houses for example redundancy cover, equity shares, mortgage subsidies and carpets or other consumer durables. Others considered that these were unnecessary gimmicks and focused on value for money in specification and high quality equipment. In yet others housing operations 'went to sleep' and staff numbers were reduced significantly – sometimes by more than 50%. Little or no land was purchased by some developers between 1989 and 1993. Housing firms had to write-down land bought from 1987 to 1989 by between 70% and 80%. The write-down of land generally started in 1990 but most firms waited until 1991 or even 1992. Those who wrote-down earlier were able to do so because they were in better financial shape and perhaps because they realised that the situation would not improve. Others went on hoping for a reversal in the market, whilst yet others were in such a difficult financial state that they dared not write-down housing and land assets in one go. Once stronger companies had acted others could follow. Many had rights issues to help absorb the consequent losses (see Chapter 3). Others, however, considered that these were just paper losses.

One company suggested that there is a limit to the size of a house-building firm. First to have sites too close together means that these would compete with each other. Secondly there is a limit to the economic size of a site because of land costs and because the time taken to develop it and the attractiveness of the development. These two factors together mean that the maximum economic size represented a relatively small market share.

On the other hand some contractors claimed that size is a favourable factor in housebuilding and that specialist housebuilders and contractors with very big housing operations are better at housing development than smaller organisations. Although very small specialist developers are successful, contractors with small housebuilding operations cannot afford the best quality management, especially if one of the corporate objectives is to balance a firm's portfolio of activities, which in turn limits the expansion of the housing business. Some contractors noted that, even though their housing operations had been very profitable, they had not reached the levels of performance achieved by the specialist housing developers. This is a judgement made with hindsight because, at the time, contractors were using their surplus cash from contracting to buy land for housing as well as borrowing from banks. As a result most expanded their housebuilding far beyond prudent levels. This view, expressed by contractors, seems to be borne out by the experienced housebuilders. Most stopped land acquisition earlier than the contractors, were generally more profitable and some were worried about too much borrowing. In the event some of the contractors have divested themselves of some or all of their housing businesses. In some cases the sell-offs were undertaken as early as 1990. In others this occurred much later, even in 1993.

Other contractors are still very involved in housing. They regard it as an attractive and controllable business, unlike commercial property development. One reason is that houses are relatively small discrete units and they can stop building when houses are not selling but they cannot stop massive property development projects. The confidence of one firm led it to operate against the trend – buying land from companies in housing receivership or distress for current or future development. Another major contractor has recently bought a local housing company. Some firms indicated that they were building houses abroad or had explored possibilities.

Generally construction companies expected housing to pick up before the contracting markets and this is already happening. Nevertheless certain constraining factors were noted. They include the phasing out of mortgage tax relief, the danger of VAT being imposed on housing, changes in attitudes of government to house price inflation – one thought that even a 5% rise in house prices could trigger a rise in the rate of interest. Another worry was land supply especially in urban areas and in the South East. In the future more sites will be on re-cycled land; green-field sites are already a rarity. Despite the difficult nature of these sites, attractive developments and profitable projects can be achieved. There is a local authority register on contaminated land. A draft law proposed that once on the register, land would never be removed from it, in case methods of decontamination improved and/or standards rose. However this legislation was not passed. Nevertheless there is a problem of obtaining insurance for projects on decontaminated land.

4.5   COMMERCIAL PROPERTY DEVELOPMENT

During the boom, there was great enthusiasm for major property developments on the part of construction companies and of banks which offered finance. Many companies borrowed and engaged in major developments which were too large for the scale of their businesses as a whole. Gearing rose substantially and whilst some of the companies managed to sell their property investments while they could still find a buyer, others were saddled with developments which they still cannot dispose of. One company withdrew from property as a pre-requisite of being taken over. In the event it divested property before the recession and so gained from this action.

Many companies have since reduced their involvement in property. However, some have decided to keep a core property expertise as a lever to gaining projects, but they are no longer prepared to use a significant amount of their own funds.

In sharp contrast to this general situation, at least two contractors regard property development as one of their core businesses which they would like to expand when the opportunity arises. One construction company, which wishes to retain its involvement in property development, insisted that its property business would not be permitted to buy land until it had developed its existing land bank. It is concentrating on fairly low risk pre-sold or pre-let developments. It has a significant steady income from retained properties and will use profits for further developments.

4.6   MINING AND MINERALS

Four out of the 18 contractors had some interest in minerals in the UK or elsewhere. These included stone, aggregates or sand and gravel and also coal and other minerals. They emphasised that the relevant skills in these businesses are knowledge and understanding of land use, surveying, planning law, ability to negotiate good contracts and to tender effectively, all of which are required in some other construction activities. The original link of contracting to opencast coal through common plant and equipment has long since disappeared. The long-term future of opencast operations was uncertain but opencast and deep mining were regarded as appropriate businesses for a construction company. Construction companies involved with these businesses are well aware of the environmental issues and the influence of the environmental lobby.

4.7   INTERNATIONAL BUSINESSES

Most of the large companies which were in international businesses saw an increase in their overseas activities as one way of overcoming the recession in the UK and, for example, one company in particular had successfully altered the relative shares of its UK and foreign businesses with the former and continental Europe now accounting for about 40% of total turnover compared with 95% in the UK alone in 1986. It is unfortunate that, during the boom conditions in the UK, many of them allowed their international business to shrink. They are now paying the price of needing to rebuild their operations overseas at a time when many other economies are coming out of recession. Some companies also acknowledged that the world market in which the UK contractors were interested was shrinking because local contractors are becoming more competent and because newly industrialised countries are increasingly involved in exporting contracting services. Moreover most contractors had burnt their fingers in international work either on a specific project abroad or in operations in a specific country and were cautious over new ventures. It is for this reason that contractors are differentiating their services, including specialising in niche markets, concentrating on sophisticated and complex projects, mainly in infrastructure, and the organisation of finance.

The traditional one-off international tenders had already fallen out of favour in 1986 and now are a very small part of international work confined to areas where companies have very special expertise or some other particular advantage. Contractors are no longer tracking UN aid or depending on ECGD. In the past, some contractors operated as local firms in particular parts of the world. This work too has declined further in importance, although some regional offices abroad are maintained. The principal use of these offices is intelligence gathering but they are very expensive to run and not very successful in competition with local businesses. Although some contractors still undertake fairly run-of-the-mill civil engineering work abroad, in general they are specialising.

When selecting markets contractors are interested in the stability of the country and the ability to get paid. Geographical location follows from that. The fast developing economies of the Far East are the most favoured location for development by many companies. Others prefer to concentrate on North America and Europe and many also operate in the Middle East. Another market is Australia where firms operate as general contractors and also offer specialised services.

Several contractors in the Far East are trying to create a demand usually by working with local firms such as consulting engineers, transportation consultants, designers and financiers. The favoured countries are Indonesia, Thailand and Hong Kong and there is increasing interest in China and other countries, such as Vietnam and Cambodia, which are slowly changing their political orientation. Malaysia was an area of great activity but at the time of writing was no longer a market for UK contractors for political reasons. One UK company is gathering data on Japanese operations in the UK and in third world countries and the way their construction industry penetrates markets but so far there is no major involvement. Companies are mostly looking for infrastructure projects including airports, railway work, ports, power generation, special water and sewerage schemes rather than building projects. These specialisms are preferred for two reasons. First, countries in the Far East are at a stage of development which requires massive investment in major civil engineering works and secondly, the hope is that once the companies have undertaken projects in these areas they will be in a good position for further work. One company however regarded the Far East as a dangerous market to get involved in and predicted that many fingers would be burnt.

Some regarded the Middle East as a reviving market for UK contractors and those which had worked in the Middle East are strengthening their operations there. In Saudi Arabia, for example, there is increased interest in private sector work partly because government settlement of accounts has been delayed. The high level of military spending has reduced available capital resources and for the first time the country has accepted a commercial loan, although this is against the principles of Islam. Contractors are also operating in Dubai, Abu Dhabi and other Gulf States through subsidiary companies, in which local firms must have a majority shareholding.

Attitudes to working in Europe are very mixed. Many companies consider that recent European Union legislation has not opened the West European market. The way in which contracts are obtained by local contractors and the participation of officials in this process often precludes fair outside competition. Some companies have linked with other European contractors for joint venture work in a third country. One has established, with three other European contractors, a company which will undertake such joint operations. Companies have also undertaken property development and housing work in Western Europe some of which has been very successful. More companies referred to plans to buy or link with European contractors in the next year or so. Nevertheless some joint operations have created nightmare situations with excessive spending on offices, as well as partners absconding with money. There was almost certainly quite inadequate management control on the part of some UK contractors investing in Europe.

Most large contractors have made connections in Eastern Europe. Some firms had entered these markets on the back of British and international clients with which they had previously worked in the UK. Others have established a reputation with international firms but have yet to penetrate local markets.

Some companies have bought an interest in former East German contracting companies. One has taken over a firm of 600 employees with an office in Berlin. It is impressed with the amount of work available in former East Germany and particularly in Berlin. One difficulty is that when purchasing the company it was required to guarantee employment for its workforce for about two years. There are problems with language for any English company. It is not politic for English speaking West Germans to manage East German companies as East Germans do not wish to be seen as subservient to West Germans. It was reported that contrary to the received wisdom, the German work force appreciates the need for hard work and discipline. It is possible that this company will develop from its base in Berlin to Poland and in the Czech and Slovak Republics. Several other contractors have set up offices in Berlin, always in conjunction with local firms. One contracting company, through its subsidiaries, is providing expert construction advice to a newly established subsidiary based in East Germany.

Another company is examining markets in Poland and other East European countries from an office in Warsaw. Yet another is in the Czech Republic. One has a well established base in the former Soviet Union and several more are investigating prospects there. One is involved in joint ventures in Turkmenistan and Kazakhstan. The problem with all these countries, including the former Soviet Union, is that whilst there is an immense need for construction projects, payment is normally in local currency and there is little hard currency available.

One country which has seen some activity and is regarded as having potential is Turkey. Several companies have undertaken civil engineering work and hotel construction, largely in joint ventures with Turkish companies. Projects tend to be major aid-assisted projects, funded internationally, or at least funded in hard currency.

Although many companies had entered North American markets in the early 1980s they withdrew for a number of reasons, including the difficulty of competing for work, the problems of controlling the management and the need to sell businesses to realise some of their capital assets. In some cases they admitted to paying too much to acquire their North American businesses. Some had persevered and are still operating in USA and Canada in mining, production of aggregates, housing, and contracting. In a few cases, especially contracting, operations have been built up from scratch. Most companies still operating in North America are planning to retain their businesses there and feel confident that they are viable in the longer term.

A number of companies operate in other parts of the world, for example, Nigeria and Zimbabwe but, in general, the view is that third world countries with very low incomes per capita are not good markets. The debts of African countries are now so substantial that international aid institutions are unwilling to lend and the situation is not helped by the human rights record of some of these countries. However at least one company was able to double turnover in Africa in 1992. There had been some interest in South America some time ago but this has faded, although a few firms are now operating there in a modest way and are optimistic about future markets.

Several companies are working in Australia across most types of business–currently including contracting, housing, railway construction and general contracting. The market for construction suffers from over-capacity and many firms are buying volume of turnover in order to obtain cash flow, as in the UK. There is very little infrastructure work. Nevertheless some see this as a key market especially as the next Olympic games are to be held in Sydney. Others have pulled out of Australia or are in the process of doing so, for example, from mining and property investment.

4.8 MARKETING POLICY

Marketing should begin with the corporate plan which ought to embody statements of what new markets the company should attempt to enter and how, what markets to withdraw from and where to increase and decrease activity. In turn this aspect of the plan should be based on a consideration of the way various markets are likely to develop and the strengths of the company in relation to them. As discussed in Chapter 6 not all contractors appreciate the way this should be done. No market plan can be 'cast in stone' because the level of demand for various products and the overall environment for different types of project vary over time in unpredictable ways. It should however be possible to plan market strategy by developing alternative scenarios depending on the level of demand in each sector. Consideration should be given to the possible effects on the company of changes in various markets, including bust or boom conditions, leading to areas for special attention in the plan.

There is a need to study the implications of the best forecasts but also to build in flexibility through considering 'what if' situations. The factors to be considered involve, for example, changes in markets, rates of interest and legislation. A sensitivity analysis should highlight areas of the company's businesses which need special attention.

There is no reason why the market plan should not include some provision for opportunities as they present themselves, for example acquisitions or joint ventures, but there should be some guidelines to the types of businesses where opportunities should be pursued. In 1986 opportunistic acquisitions and developments were one of the features of the management of companies. An essential element in developing a view of future markets must be the exploration of different scenarios leading to assessment of the chances of threatening consequences. It was this part of the planning process which some of the companies interviewed felt most uncomfortable with – familiarisation with the unfamiliar.

Had the companies which were planning in the boom conditions of the mid and late 1980s thought the unthinkable, for example, a collapse in the property or housing markets, they should have been able to avoid some of the disastrous consequences of the recession. Perhaps they should now be thinking about the consequences of future volatile interest rates and possibly higher inflation as well as about changes required during a recovery or even a further recession.

The way in which markets are analysed must not be confined to types of buildings and structures since the company also needs to consider the type of contractual arrangements, whether it can offer additional services to achieve a competitive advantage, where the greatest value-added can be achieved and where it wishes to operate geographically. All the companies interviewed were doing this to some degree (see Chapter 5). The packaging of the services offered has become an increasing element in their marketing strategy.

Clearly much of the market analysis has to come from those who are close to the markets such as the regional offices of the national firms, but there is also a place for a group overview. Some companies have economists and others whose task it is to set the scene. They too have to think in terms of various scenarios.

In those companies which did not have an effective corporate plan and therefore no clear objectives, marketing managers found it hard to project a clear company image or to structure their work.

Several companies have a marketing manager or an executive with a similar title. Often he takes the output of the planning process through to implementation and uses his initiative to develop ideas of what markets the company should be operating in. In other companies this function is fulfilled by senior line managers. As the trend is towards decentralization, in many companies the divisional boards regard themselves as heading almost autonomous companies including being in charge of their own marketing in the broadest sense. Within a regional division in one company a senior management meeting is held monthly to decide policy on contracts. Based on reports from two (formerly three) marketing staff and on information from the client, they pin-point the type of work they wish to tender for by type, size and area. This is undertaken against the background of the three year plan. The selling is done through high level contacts with potential clients. But at the other extreme it is carried out by sales staff who investigate potential leads.

Where both the Head Office and divisions have a marketing function, the Head Office marketing manager usually has a role of information coordinator, meeting the divisional marketing managers at regular intervals to discuss issues which span several divisions and initiatives in different sectors, to exchange information generally and to standardise group policy.

As a separate matter the marketing manager might participate in the planning of the tactics for obtaining each contract opportunity up to the point at which tender documents come in. He also might have a role of forecaster of markets using existing published sources or making his own independent assessments. In addition, the marketing manager could be responsible for public relations both externally and internally and the production of company brochures and newsletters as well as for publicity on successful projects. Such publications have improved dramatically in recent years.

Generally an understanding by the main board of markets and marketing has improved since the mid 1980s. Because of the increased role and influence of clients, members of the industry are more aware of those factors which affect decisions to build and, because of the lack of building work, it has become essential for firms to spend time improving their knowledge of their markets. Further, firms are more sensitive in approaching and working with prospective clients than in the past and are prepared to invest heavily in this process. Whereas in the early 1980s there was no inkling that it would be possible to create work, now construction companies are beginning to initiate ideas for projects which may lead to construction work especially with major public clients or privatised corporations. In almost all cases selling to a prospective client begins at a much earlier stage.

Projecting the right profile of the business is seen as an important element of the marketing process. A divisional director of one large company said that its image had been changed from civil engineering and local authority housing to imaginative projects generally including retail developments, city centres and industrial work. 'It is necessary to show that the company has flair and charisma' he said.

Another stressed that marketing is a different business from even ten years ago. 'In those days one always entertained and met people. Now you are dealing with professionals and there is a need for more imaginative marketing and it is vital to show more technical knowledge. You may hire the Orient Express to entertain but in the end you have to sell your product on merit. During the recession it is necessary to run even faster to stay still'.

The majority of the firms interviewed now have well-considered marketing strategies – a great improvement on say five years ago – although the marketing of some firms is still rudimentary. In a number of companies the role of the marketing manager remains ill-defined and is still of relatively low status. Consequently the marketing manager is not part of the core management team. The information to help marketing managers fulfil either function has been considerably bolstered but the resources under his control are modest and confirm the ambiguous nature of marketing in construction companies.

In general, however, there is a much clearer understanding than in the mid 1980s of the respective roles of heads of divisional and group operations in the marketing of company services and in the background role of the marketing managers.

Reference

1. Geroski, Paul and Gregg, Paul 'Corporate Restructuring in the UK during the Recession', *Business Strategy Review*, Vol. 5, No. 2, Summer 1994, pp. 1–19.

5 Marketing Contracting Services

5.1 INTRODUCTION

There have been substantial improvements in the innovative and flexible approach of contracting companies selling their expertise and services. Because of the recession contractors have been forced to explore every possible way of obtaining work to maintain their turnover. This has been reinforced by the emphasis on core businesses of which contracting is the most important. They have done this by broadening the existing services they offer and by offering new services or new ways of supplying services.

After Section 5.2 which gives an overall view of the importance of various responses, Section 5.3 of this chapter deals with the first category and explains how contractors have developed their regional activities in the UK (5.3.1) and abroad (5.3.2). They have also obtained work from receivers of failed companies (5.3.3) and have devoted effort to improving the quality of their services (5.3.4).

Section 5.4 covers the ways in which they have developed new services such as new forms of contractual arrangements (5.4.1), provision of finance for projects (5.4.2) or have extended their business forward into the process or created niche markets (5.4.3). Sometimes they have linked with other contractors to reduce risk or increase expertise (5.4.4).

5.2 RESPONSE OF COMPANIES TO RECESSION

Some idea of the range of responses of companies to the recession in the area of contracting operations is shown in Table 5.1 (p. 78). These are compared with the response of companies in British industry as a whole to the recession as found by Geroski and Gregg[1] in a study of some 600 firms. The reactions of the construction companies were generally those not applicable to UK industry as a whole but it will be seen that while some companies did make acquisitions they were on a small

77

Table 5.1 Contracting market-related actions taken in response to recession
during the period 1989–93

Action	Construction companies in survey		UK industry generally
	%	Rank	%
Acquire other companies	18	8=	23
Develop overseas markets	47	5=	52
Develop special expertise in markets	53	4	na
Involvement in earlier and later stages of projects	47	5=	na
Acquire projects from defunct companies	18	8=	na
Put equity into projects	41	7	na
Take on smaller contracts	82	3	na
Put in lower bid prices	88	1=	na
Bid for more projects	88	1=	na

Sources: Geroski, P.A. and Gregg, P., 'Coping with Recession', *National Institute Economic Review,* November 1993, pp. 64–75, and interviews.

scale and there were no mergers. Those companies which were in overseas businesses did generally want to expand there but not all companies were so involved.

Details of the mechanism for some of these changes are given in the sections which follow.

5.3 EXTENSION OF EXISTING SERVICES

5.3.1 Developing regional penetration

Some of the larger contractors have been reducing the number of their regional offices in order to reduce overheads but they have often kept sub-offices because a local presence is generally regarded as important. Some other companies, mainly smaller ones, have actually increased their regional coverage during the recession. Construction is basically a personal business and a local office encourages trust between client and contractor and hopefully a stream of orders especially from repeat clients. Regional managers considered that one of the major advantages of a regional office compared with their medium sized local competition was that they could understand local markets and become 'a friendly local builder' yet they had access to the most advanced project management techniques, technical advice from head office and the security provided from being part of a national organisation. This is often the case when undertaking projects under new forms of contract. Once a regional office has obtained a local client there tends to be a more stable long-term client relationship and negotiated work may be obtained. This is helped because many regional offices have small works departments and so are able to service their clients on a continuing basis. It is not easy for a national contractor to establish itself on a local basis. Developing effective relationships and trust takes time. Local clients need to be reassured that the regional office of a national firm will continue in the longer term.

At times when business is poor there is a temptation for regional managers to secure work at lower margins to ensure sufficient workload to justify the existence of the office. If workload fell dramatically the group could restructure its operations by closing down some regional offices and servicing areas from other offices. This contrasted with the approach of local firms which was to shrink with the market. The implication was that regional offices were liable to take more risks when bidding for work than local firms largely as a means of ensuring continued employment for regional staff.

Regional differences also affect labour and other practices and in some areas of the country it is virtually essential to have a local office to obtain work and even to execute it. A notable area is Liverpool which for decades has been a very tightly controlled local market. It is also important to have local offices in Scotland and Wales.

In the late 1980s major contractors gave considerable freedom to recently acquired regional companies to carry on with their existing style of management and to keep their independence. One company which was a strong advocate of this policy in 1986 has now brought these local companies more under the control of the parent and is using the group image as well as local company names to promote itself and obtain business. Nevertheless there are clearly advantages in keeping local names – a policy which is still followed by some companies.

5.3.2   Expanding work abroad

A response from a number of contractors to the falling workload in the United Kingdom has been to undertake more contracting work abroad. Of the companies interviewed five of the smaller ones were not operating overseas and did not wish to do so but of the large contractors all said that they wished to increase their overseas turnover. A number acknowledged that the amount of work available to expatriate contractors around the world was likely to decrease. Thus, it is likely that not all contractors will be successful in achieving their objectives of expanding overseas work. It is partly for this reason that many of the larger contractors are differentiating their services and offering services which are beyond the construction process such as finance and the management of the facilities. International work as a whole is discussed fully in Section 4.7.

5.3.3   Taking over contracts from companies in receivership

Several contractors have taken over companies in receivership or shared in the workload and order books of others in severe difficulties. In some cases they took over unfinished contracts from bankrupt companies. One company in particular acquired a number of contracts in this way, such that it developed a method for the assessment of companies in difficulties and outstanding contracts which could be applied over a weekend. Until recently a fortnight was the usual period within which they had to assess and bid for parts of bankrupt companies so that quick decisions by would-be purchasers were crucial.

There is however a problem in taking over a company which is in difficulty. The Transfer of Undertaking (Protection of Employment) Regulations 1981 (TUPE) states that if a firm is acquired and the purchaser wishes to reduce the number of employees, then he has to accord full redundancy and pension rights to the acquired employees according to their rights in their previous employment. Thus the acquiring company has an enormous potential liability for redundancy and other severance payments. If the Department of Employment, for example, paid out money to those who were initially made redundant but were then reemployed, the Department could ask the contractor to reimburse the money it had paid out. Another area of concern was the pension rights of persons employed in a now defunct company, since the acquiring company could be liable for pensions earned in the acquired company. An instance was quoted of a national company which took over a large regional company and was required effectively to pay additional sums, in excess of £100,000 for that company.

These liabilities and risks of liability discourage takeovers. Companies therefore prefer taking on contracts where they can employ just a few of the original staff. It is important not to take on the head office of the bankrupt company as this is considered as taking the whole company over. The acquiring companies regretted that they could not take over the businesses as a whole but, as they did not need all of the new staff, they were unable to take any other course of action but to acquire only individual projects. The ability to take on individual contracts is an obvious advantage in construction, compared with purchases from receivers in other industries where processes do not lend themselves to fragmented disposal of assets or work in progress.

Takeovers from central and local government were excluded from the provisions of TUPE but from 1 September 1993 the scope of the law was widened to include non-commercial activities.

One problem with this method of obtaining work is the speed with which a company must act to assess another company with a large number of contracts, the need to review many records and forecast the income from contracts and the costs of completion. There are a number of factors to be considered in evaluating a contract, say, half way through. The valuation must take account of the work carried out and not paid for, claims for damages if the work was not satisfactory and increases in cost if a project was bid at a loss. There is a vast amount of work for accountants, for example on the tax positions, for lawyers and surveyors. In housebuilding the calculation is more straightforward because a company is buying an asset without any contractual obligations.

The client has the right to give the contract to another contractor. However, if a contract has been taken over at the same price to the client, he is usually happy with the arrangement provided he is convinced of the acquiring company's capability.

A company which had acquired several contracts in this way said that the opportunity to do so in 1993 was less than in previous years and the competition to acquire them greater, as other contractors realised that this was a beneficial way of obtaining work. Indeed some considered that to take-over a number of contracts from a company, as well as some key staff, was a cheaper and quicker way of increasing their size than organic growth because they could acquire an organisation at below current value. However not all of their experiences were successful. Other companies, indeed, regarded acquisitions of companies and contracts in this way as very risky because it takes time to evaluate the real value. They thought that the number of contractors interested in a failed company and queuing to examine its books was quite extraordinary.

5.3.4   Improvement of quality

The British Standards Institution Quality Assurance Standard, BS5750, has been adopted by some of the construction companies interviewed and some of those already registered are looking towards European Quality Registration in 1994. It is reported to be necessary to be registered under BS5750 to obtain certain types of contracts and some contractors expect to be able to obtain more negotiated contracts as a result. However it is acknowledged that quality within the organisation which influences the efficiency of projects is much deeper than required by BS5750. This is only the foundation for good quality; it demonstrates that systems are in place for controlling the business and the site. It was reported that some site managers were very enthusiastic about its introduction. One of the smaller companies interviewed reckoned that preparation for registration cost about a quarter of a million pounds. The projection of the image of the company in terms of quality is one of the ways contractors are trying to obtain more profitable work. However no instances have been found where contractors have obtained more work because of quality assurance.

Some contractors are considering the application of value management and value engineering to the way they run projects and parts of their business. A few firms have arranged training of their managers in this approach and hope to use it to improve the quality of their service and of the finished product. (For definitions and discussion see Green.)[2]

5.4   NEW SERVICES AND NEW WAYS OF SUPPLYING EXISTING SERVICES

5.4.1   Design and build and other non-traditional contracts

There has been a major shift away from traditional contracts. The present fashion is to move towards design and build which has led a number of companies to shift managerial resources to strengthen capability under this type of contract. This approach is seen by clients to offer a less complicated approach to procurement with single point contact and, for some projects, guaranteed prices. There are two types of design and build contract. The first is where the contractor employs his own in-house architect or a firm of architects to undertake the design under his control and then carries out the construction. The second type is where the initial design is already undertaken by an architect employed by the client and the client asks the contractor to take over the responsibility for the detailed design and the construction of the project. This second approach is referred to as novated design and build, that is, the contract between the architect and the client is taken over by the contractor from the client. The contractors employ the architects who have produced the initial designs. Recent surveys by Akintoye[3] and MBD[4] have suggested that in 1993 novated design and build accounted for about one half of all design and build contracts in the UK despite being resented by many in the industry.

Some companies have in-house design teams, others do not. All rely to some extent on independent architects and design practices. Although some firms specialise in particular types of work, design and build services cover the full range of building and civil engineering work including water treatment plants, hospitals and roads. This is one of the reasons why some firms need to employ external designers. They cannot maintain a sufficient flow of work for their own directly employed specialist designers. Some firms have closed their design offices, partly because of the need for specialist skills which the firms cannot afford to maintain in-house, partly because of the recession and also because some architects exclude contractors which have in-house design teams from tender lists.

Several firms claimed that design and build provided one of the most effective ways of reducing building times and gave impressive examples of the reduction in time and cost of building shopping centres, industrial facilities and commercial premises. This was especially the case when they worked with regular clients whose standards and approach to business were well understood and where there was a close rapport with the professionals employed by the client. Clients have confirmed the benefits of such close working relationships in achieving fast building times. A few companies were able to obtain over 50% of their work from long-term continuing clients, much on a negotiated basis. Continuing clients have been able to insist on faster building and reduced costs. It was reported that over a period of six years, building times for some projects, for example out-of-town developments, have been reduced by two-thirds and costs have also been reduced significantly. However this is, no doubt, also partly due to recessionary slack right across the industry. Some fast track work, particularly shop fitting for major retailers and banks, provided a quick turnover and although margins were not high it was seen as relatively risk free.

The reported advantages of design and build to clients were that conflict was reduced; there were no major surprises; responsibilities for design and construction were not split and the original price was more likely to be adhered to. The contractor, who has more assets than the architects, is liable for the design although unlike the architect he does not always carry professional indemnity insurance.

There is a diversity of views about the merits of novated design and build. One company resented the additional risk in taking over an existing design because the contractor was responsible for its quality and felt that it was then often too late to improve the method of construction. Other contractors were in favour of novated design and build contracts because they gave the client the opportunity to decide on requirements at pre-tender stage. Having established an outline design and a standard these clients normally did not change their minds. It also gave the contractor control over the architect. There were no client claims for lack of detailed information and the system allowed the contractor to work closely with the architect to influence the detailed design. Moreover the novated method had lower overheads because less design work was involved for the contractor. The problem of liability was covered by professional indemnity insurance held by the contractor. One contractor said he was insured for disasters but the policy had a high limit and also a large excess. In the highly competitive situation of the recession a novated contract was preferred. On the other hand if it was possible to negotiate a design and build contract, the full design and build approach was more advantageous because the contractor had more control, could use his own expertise to his own advantage and more value was added.

Management contracting, which was favoured in the 1980s, has declined in importance although some firms had obtained a lot of work under this approach. In one company it was down, by the end of 1993, to nearly a tenth of previous levels. The experience of others was similar. Companies which had set up specific units to run management contracts had closed them down, mainly because of the decline in demand but also because the greater flexibility and familiarity of staff with this type of work meant that it was not necessary to distinguish it within the organisation from traditional or other forms of contract. Nevertheless some contractors still have substantial management contracting commitments. Although the return on these contracts is not high and the cash generated low, their main advantage is that they are less risky than other forms of contract.

Construction management contracts are no longer very significant in number. This may be because of the decline in commercial projects where the application of this approach appears to be most appropriate.

It is important to manage the size of contracts in any portfolio of projects. One company which anticipated a serious recession early in the downturn succeeded in obtaining some very large contracts to produce work over a period of years. At the other extreme, in late 1993, firms were very cautious about taking contracts of long duration because of the fear that, even with a slight upturn, materials and labour costs might rise.

5.4.2 Provision of finance and financial packages

Contractors used a lot of ingenuity in finding work in a period of intense competition, and hence in seeking workload and profit. One way was to operate across a broader range of stages of the project. In contrast to traditional styles of marketing, when contractors either waited to be invited to tender or developed their contacts to achieve nomination or to get onto tender lists, contractors now realize that they have to capitalise on their special expertise and take a very proactive marketing stance.

Basically they have sought ways to differentiate their services from other competing contractors. This has been achieved in various ways including extension of the project backwards before the construction phase; putting together financial packages and identifying potential projects; by forward extension to include: equipping and furnishing a project, the maintenance of the building or structure and the management of the facility; as well as by offering different ways of managing the construction project.

A few contractors identified projects in the UK and overseas which appeared to be viable even before the prospective client had recognised a need for these projects. For example a contracting company might identify a piece of land which could be better used by an owner, even though there might be some existing facility on that site; or it might propose the construction of an airport to some administrative authority, for example, in Eastern Europe, which had not envisaged that development. It then worked with the prospective client to develop a scheme in anticipation that it would be awarded the contract. These opportunities tended to arise when the client was inexperienced in development or had previously been involved in a narrow range of work. For example, contractors have worked with some recently privatised public sector organisations and with organisations in countries with rapidly changing economies.

Rather more companies became involved with projects after clients had identified a need. They helped to explore possible approaches to a project and how it should be structured and funded. The range of expertise available at this stage within some contractors is extensive and covers more than property development and construction aspects. Firms have developed extensive skills in the businesses of clients for whom they eventually undertake construction projects, such as: health, water, airports, power generation, and light railways.

To operate effectively in these niche markets, firms needed to develop a total capability including specification, designing, equipping a building for full operation, operating and maintaining. As a result some firms had to recruit specialists in a number of fields, for example, medical specialists for hospital projects. To some extent this became desirable, and possible, because of the changes taking place in the public sector in the UK. However, it was only with this very detailed knowledge that the advice of contractors was likely to be heeded by clients who were at an early stage in developing a scheme. For credibility the firms had to demonstrate complete mastery of the business area.

The key to developing a project lies in identifying and securing finance. In the mid 1980s contractors were active in facilitating and helping clients identify and access sources of finance. This was particularly prevalent for large overseas projects and at that time contractors were increasingly employing specialised staff to undertake this function. Though in the mid 1980s there were major departures from past practice, the approach is now quite common for UK projects. Some contractors increasingly take equity in the schemes. It has become more usual because contractors are so desperate for work that they are prepared to be flexible in helping companies obtain finance to ensure that a project goes ahead.

Introducing private finance into public projects has become very important because government has cut down the availability of finance for public sector infrastructure projects and is attempting to involve the private sector. There is greater autonomy in raising finance in those units which were in the former public sector. Increasingly the projects for which contractors are finding finance are: design – build – own – operate projects or some version of this type of arrangement. If the contractor takes some equity, it virtually ensures that he obtains the construction contract. Secondly, it shows commitment on the part of the contractor to the total project. Thirdly, it provides an income flow to the contractor independent of fluctuations in the construction industry. Most companies taking equity want to be able to dispose of that equity if necessary. Also, they insist that both parts of a project – the construction and the operation of the facility – should be viable. It is regarded as very important for firms to have their own technical, legal and financial experts before going into these projects.

There has been considerable criticism of the attitude of the British Government to private financing and infrastructure projects. The contractor in these types of arrangement contributes to the design and construction of the project and operates the built facilities until a defined level of income is achieved whereupon the facility is transferred to government ownership. The problem is that with this method the contractor takes the risk that the project might not produce the income required to achieve the transfer, but does not get a corresponding gain if the income exceeds this level.

There are two types of risk. One is that the operating costs are higher than expected – the operator can accept this risk because to some extent it is in his control. However the risk that the project will not be wanted at all is not a risk an operator can take – for example that the prison system is replaced by an alternative or that a prison built with private finance is not needed. Another example is that a new motorway financed by a toll is not used by enough vehicles.

The idea of shadow tolls is imaginative but they are difficult to assess and administer. In addition, for any one project several contractors are expected to spend a significant amount of money putting up a scheme which might be subject to planning delays or delays in offering the contract because of government indecision. The amounts involved in developing a scheme are large, six figures were mentioned by several companies. One suggestion is that the government should itself undertake the design of the project which is then put out to tender for build, own, and manage, with possible later transfer. In many European countries the contractors are reimbursed for some of the design costs. A similar move might take place in the UK.

Some of the problems are being dealt with by the Private Finance Panel set up by the Treasury under the Chairmanship of Sir Alastair Morton. In any case some improvements have been made since most of the interviews were carried out. For example, private finance guidelines were issued in March 1994 by DoE after consultation with the industry. The new rules limit the number of bidders to three or four; allow compensation if a project cannot proceed for reasons outside the control of bidders; and state that, wherever possible, departments should give a commitment to a definite timetable. The guidelines also ask departments to state clearly the risks they want to share with the private sector, and permit them to let contracts without tendering in exceptional circumstances. Finally, compensation is to be paid to unsuccessful bidders if their ideas are incorporated into the winning scheme.

Nowadays the British Government is in competition with other international projects to obtain funds for infrastructure projects. For example a potential financial sponsor might be considering, on the one hand, a second Severn crossing and, on the other, a water supply project in Indonesia. However, compared with a few years ago at the height of Thatcherism, when government would not even contemplate some public funding, there is now a greater opportunity to involve the public sector, especially for projects which because of the level of risk or return would otherwise be of marginal viability.

The construction company/operator must have a good return and a way out of his investment but the UK government does not seem to have realised that this ability to sell the development to some other investor or operator is important. Ultimately there is a need to create an investing public, probably institutions, to finance these types of projects. This is the way to provide a contractor with an exit route for his investment.

5.4.3   New forms of diversification and specialisation

Some of the diversifications of the 1980s were soundly based with a link of expertise between construction and the new venture. Others were purely opportunistic and in areas of business where the contractor had no previous experience. Some of the failures of diversification in the 1980s were the result of poor management in the control of the acquired businesses. In the boom it was difficult not to make a profit but as soon as the boom was over the weaknesses in acquired companies showed themselves.

The first problem was that some of the new businesses disturbed the balance between cash hungry and cash generating parts of the organisation. For example, some businesses, including plant hire, are cash hungry and at least one company was unable to provide sufficient investment for a newly acquired plant business. Secondly, the existing management of the acquired companies was often retained, virtually intact, partly to keep the advantages of the past reputation and goodwill. However, the control of that existing management was often inadequate. Sometimes it appeared that the new business was efficient because it was profitable but with the effects of the recession it soon became unprofitable. At the same time a number of acquisitions had led to top-heavy boards because directors from some of the newly acquired businesses secured a seat on the parent company board.

Most contractors (but not quite all) said they would not go into unconnected businesses again. Now, although firms are reducing their level of diversification, it is nevertheless taking place in other ways.

One type is facilities management. Speedy access to this has been made easier by the sale of parts of the Property Services Agency – the five regional businesses involved in maintaining government estates, many of them primarily concerned with Ministry of Defence work. It is envisaged that there will be much work in this field in, for example, local authorities, universities, hospitals, schools and water companies. It is mainly fee based.

Housing Association business has grown rapidly in the last few years although contractors doubt that that market will continue to be as advantageous as it has been in the past few years. Contractors assist with land search, planning approval and construction but do not substantially invest their own cash.

Several companies mentioned transportation, especially new methods for the movement of people, for example light railways, metros and more traditional railways, but this is an international rather than a domestic market. One contractor in particular was concentrating attention on this area. The railway business seems to be blossoming in several parts of the world compared with a decade earlier. It involves not only track laying but also overhead electrification, the production of sleepers, ballast and often other track components. Work is going on in Australia, South Africa and South East Asia.

Other areas of work are energy projects, health facilities, and airports. The development of these niche markets can give contractors a reputation for expertise in fairly complex fields so that it is easier to be able to negotiate contracts in these areas or at least be invited to tender. This is linked to the financing and operating of facilities (see Section 5.4.2) and to international work (Section 4.7) For example, in order to obtain major infrastructure and other project work, contractors invest in projects and often operate the facilities which they have developed. They are, therefore, diversifying, acquiring assets in and managing other businesses. Developments which are either in the process of being pursued or being considered include: telephone systems, airports, hospitals, power stations, transport facilities, prisons, water and sewerage systems. The diversity of these businesses raises the question of whether the companies have sufficient expertise to control them. The contractors often reply that success depends on having the right partner who is able to run the newly constructed operation. A good joint venture will make the operating partner wholly responsible to the client so that if the partner goes out of business there is no redress to the contractor.

These new businesses provide an income flow independent of the construction cycle. The contractors claim that they would not undertake this type of work unless they gained a profit from both the construction project and from the investment in the facility. Some companies already have a significant income flow from these operations.

Most of those interviewed gave a conventional view of the nature of construction markets and the determinants of demand and offered little about how these might change, except in terms of demographic factors, such as population age profiles, the level of industrialisation and consumer affluence. Generally the relationships implied by these views do seem appropriate for markets in many developing countries and in, say, Eastern Europe. However, they may not hold for markets in mature western economies. For example, whilst the impact of the use of IT on the design of commercial buildings was appreciated, the longer term implications such as the substitution of communication technologies for the physical workplace housed in, say, an office building was not being considered. There were exceptions. One company was exploring the application of advanced communications technologies in the work-place. Its aim was understanding the nature of the office of 2010 and developing its businesses around the opportunities which might arise. Overall, however, there were few strong views about what would drive the market for construction in UK and Europe over the next ten years.

5.4.4 Links with other contractors

The smaller of the companies interviewed were interested in forming joint ventures with other contractors to undertake bigger projects, for example road works. Indeed even the largest contractors have a certain limit on the value of any one contract they would undertake without a joint venture because they want to limit exposure to risk. In some cases joint ventures with companies from mainland Europe for UK projects were set up as a way of tapping into expertise and capital without necessitating a link with rival UK ones. There are advantages both to the client and the UK partner as it ensures a stronger competitive element.

References

1. Geroski P.A., and Gregg, P., 'Coping with Recession', *National Institute Economic Review,* November 1993, pp. 64–75.
2. Green, Stuart D., 'Beyond value engineering: SMART value management for building projects', *International Journal of Project Management,* 1994, 12 (1) pp. 49–56.
3. Akintoye, A., 'Design and build: a survey of contractors' views', *Construction Management and Economics,* Vol. 12, No. 2 pp. 155–63.
4. MBD, *The UK Design and Build Market Development* (MBD, 1994).

6 Structure, Management Methods and Planning

6.1 INTRODUCTION

Section 6.2 of this chapter considers the advantages and disadvantages of being a public limited company which was the case for the majority of the companies interviewed (6.2.1). It goes on to examine companies' problems of structure and management which existed earlier but became obvious during the recession. Many of those interviewed related organisational changes to the recommendations in the Cadbury Report[1] (6.2.2).

Section 6.3 deals with corporate planning and compares managers' attitudes to planning in the 1990s recession with that adopted in earlier recessions (6.3.1 and 6.3.2). The vital importance of communication, implementation and monitoring of the plans is discussed in Section 6.3.3.

6.2 STRUCTURE

6.2.1 Type of company

The introduction to this volume shows that thirteen of the eighteen companies were quoted public limited companies, three were owned by UK public limited companies or foreign companies and two were private limited companies. Five of the public limited companies and two of the private limited companies were family controlled or effectively so. In 1986 a further one would have been similarly described. There have been changes in their formal and informal structure over the last eight years.

One company had been floated as a public limited company in the late 1980s and another one had major shareholdings by a family trust but these were then sold on the Stock Exchange. Family firms which are public limited companies or companies where the control is virtually exercised by a trust are somewhat protected from the markets. These two companies were thus fully exposed for the first time to the public and Stock Exchange scrutiny of their activities. There were other companies which still had a clear memory of the effects of transferring from a limited liability company to a public limited company and yet others which are considering the change.

The advantages of being a public company, and hence some of the reasons for going public, were stated as follows:

● it is the only way to create a market value for shares;
● it enables the family shareholders to assess the value of their holdings and to realise some of their investments for use in other ways or to buy other investments to spread risk;
● it enables the company to raise new money from the market and to expand;
● it facilitates the issues of shares to directors and managers who are not family members;
● it shifts decision-making from being family-centred to being management-led;
● it helps to impress banks and hence permits greater borrowing and expansion;
● it develops contacts with leading city figures;
● it is beneficial to marketing to be seen as a public company with a higher profile than a private company;
● monitoring of performance and comparison with competitors increases efficiency.

The disadvantages are that:

● the costs of bringing the company to the Stock Exchange are huge;
● it brings the company into the limelight and if the company faces bad results its share price drops;
● poor Stock Exchange ratings are disturbing to clients and workers and could lead to a takeover;
● the 'quiet life' of a limited company must be given up;
● there is great pressure to maintain dividends at reasonable levels;
● the need regularly to discuss the state of the company with analysts and to keep shareholders informed is burdensome;
● the short-termism of the stock market may lead to inappropriate actions and the company no longer has the freedom of action for its longer term health.

One company concluded that in bad times it is better to be a private company whereas in good times it is preferable to be a public company. The company where the major family trust had sold out its holdings experienced changes which were judged largely beneficial. It became subject to external pressures and had to consider the effect of its actions on its share price. Previously dividends were high and they were cut to the level of the sector. The company needed to perform better and to be more informative to its shareholders and to be more open generally. Also it was enabled to raise money without protests from the controlling shareholder. With hindsight the company had under-performed for two decades due to the conservative policies of the trust and lack of external pressures to do better. Steps are being taken to rectify the situation.

Family firms have had a major part to play in the development of the construction industry and even in 1988 half of the top 35 firms in the industry were of this type in the sense that either the combined family-related shareholdings effectively gave them financial control or a number of directors were members of the same family and held management control. Since that time family control has been reduced in both senses. One of the reasons why families retained control of very substantial companies was that they had been able to grow organically without the need for large injections of capital. However, it is likely that in the future companies will need more capital assets even for relatively straightforward contracting. The tendency is for banks to lend only against a reasonable level of assets and for large clients to scrutinise the accounts of contractors to satisfy themselves that assets are adequate. The increase in bonding requires an increase in capital. It is also easier to raise money on the stock market if the company has high asset values. Lastly the contracting companies are taking equity in various schemes for which they need access to funds.

Many of the companies with a large number of family members on the board were founded or grew large over 50 years ago. The family is often second, third or even fourth generation. The chances that there will be a continuing supply of family members able and willing to manage the business recedes with time and in many cases has already proved impossible to attain. The days of a number of large family controlled companies in the industry are numbered.

6.2.2 Structure and management within the company

A number of problems experienced by companies at the beginning of the recession were quoted during interviews. Many of these existed during to the boom but became only too apparent during the recession. They included:

- several separate construction divisions without a common policy;
- failing to make the best use of cash generated;
- overmanning at the top with duplication of management functions;
- overlarge boards fragmented into a number of separate interest groups;
- board meetings at which inadequate control over the various businesses was exercised and no action agreed;
- too many minor business activities;
- failure to appreciate the management problems of businesses recently acquired and to deal with them;
- inadequate control over capital expenditure on land acquisition;
- excessive emphasis on profit and loss accounts at the expense of adequate monitoring of adverse balance sheet developments including failure to maintain a register of group properties;
- neglect of international markets because of the UK boom.

The large contracting companies are however changing rapidly in their methods of management. One interviewee referred to the dynasties amongst the large contractors. Some of the large family companies are amongst the very best but others were referred to as gentlemanly and, in a few cases, old fashioned and autocratic. The few to which this applied have been finally forced by the recession to change to a different management style and also to a tougher less paternalistic attitude.

Change has occurred partly because the boards of some of these companies did not provide for the development of top class managers within the companies and they were forced to recruit from outside. This often led to a more structured management hierarchy and a change of image of the company with a more outward-looking approach. Such change has been essential to managing the recession and planning for the future.

Several senior managers considered that over a long period of time the lack of controls and sloppy management structures were partly responsible for their difficulties during the recession. The boom masked the situation because of the high level of profits. During the recession companies have been driven to rethink their structure. This is because of earlier failures, in some cases by top management, to control the activities of all parts of their businesses, and by the need to reduce overheads to survive. The result has been changes, many of which apply across a whole range of companies.

First, the main boards of many companies have been reduced in size. During the boom years, boards grew; with the appointment of chief executives of companies which had been acquired – often part of the takeover deal; with the appointment of heads of divisions, even if their general group management skills were not equal to this role; with the appointment of members of staff with the object of retaining their services in a very buoyant management labour market; and lastly with the appointment of non-executive directors who had some relevant influence – often political or financial. These large boards could not properly control the various facets of the business and in the boom, when profits were easily made, there was a complacency which enabled companies to operate with quite inadequate information about the performance of various new and existing businesses. Moreover too many board members were fighting for their own particular part of the business rather than taking a group view.

Main boards have been slimmed down, sometimes to about half their previous size, typically eight but with a range of five to eleven. This has been helped by the divestment of some activities. It was found that the smaller board is more flexible and because all members are group-oriented little time is wasted by members defending their own particular interest. However, one chief executive recognised that the number of full-time executives on the main board had been cut back too sharply and there was now a need to groom one or two senior members of the company for the board appointment. In a few companies the chairman also has the role of chief executive. This is contrary to the spirit of the Cadbury Committee[2] which states that in principle the chairman's role should be separate from that of the chief executive.

A factor which is leading to the enlargement of boards, however, is the recommendation of the Cadbury Committee that the number of non-executive directors should be at least three. There were mixed feelings as to whether this was right and some companies had not fully implemented this recommendation. In 1993 about a third of board members of plcs in the study were non-executive but in six companies, including two companies which were subsidiaries, there were fewer than three non-executive directors. However, it was felt that the proposal in the Cadbury Report that non-executives should consider pensions and remuneration of board members was right. There were complaints that too many papers and too much time in board meetings was devoted to keeping non-executive directors up-to-date. One senior director commented that the structure of a major company does not matter 'as long as you have the right people'. He believes in a flat pyramid. 'People at the pit face run the company'. But with reference to the Cadbury recommendations not being fully implemented he said that 'if a company has too many non-executive directors it creates distancing and complexity in decision-making rather than checks and balances which is the purpose'.

However some companies have selected non-executive directors carefully for their special skills and were very satisfied with their choice and with the functioning of the board as a whole. There seems to have been a slight shift in the perceived role of non-executive directors from political influence and wide-ranging contacts to particular skills and knowledge vital to the development of the company in its new chosen direction.

It was thought important that non-executive members should have opportunities for discussions and consultation with executive directors outside formal meetings and to meet senior staff. The Chairman must avert the danger of the board splitting into executive and non-executive directors in policy matters. In about half of the companies the chairman was a non-executive director.

In general, boards were found to be performing better after the improvements of the past few years, with more than half rated as functioning well and only one or two functioning poorly.

An approach being tried in one company is to have a few associate directors who meet several times a year to consider main board papers and financial data and who prepare reports at the request of the main board. It is a training ground for board directors, facilitates the sifting process and smooths the transition from running a subsidiary company to taking a group view. 'One of them will float to the top', that is, to the PLC board.

In some companies the Board has executive committees with delegated authority. This overcomes the problem of handling important decisions which need to be taken between main board meetings. The committee normally consists of key executive members of the main board though in one company the personnel director – not a member of the main board – is also a member.

Both board meetings and executive committees receive a much higher quality of information than a few years ago. This is due to rationalisation of financial data to achieve better financial controls, to improved project reports and better knowledge of market trends coupled with senior managers' determination to avoid the disasters of the recent past. The functioning of boards has been facilitated by recent developments in the use of information technology. Companies are better able to select the type of system best suited to their needs and some companies have invested heavily in improved systems during the recession. Information technology now covers most aspects of the business – estimating, planning, design and engineering procurement but most importantly financial control and accounting, where systems have been refined to produce not only speedier and more accurate information but also more relevant information. This has led to a reduction in accounting and other staff.

The structure of the subsidiary boards has changed similarly to those of the main board. It is considered essential in most companies to have one executive director of the main board on each subsidiary board. In one company with few subsidiaries four main board members attended most of the subsidiary company board meetings – the chairman attended about 95% of them. Responsibility for each company was allocated to a board member who reports on that company to the main board.

There are different problems in the management of overseas subsidiaries or jointly owned companies in all countries but especially where there are language, cultural or legal differences. It is essential for the parent company board to have proper control of the operations of the overseas company. However to insist that senior management should be from the UK may well mean the loss of the trust of the local management, resulting in a lack of communication and an inadequate flow of information. It is essential to have monthly financial reviews, monitoring of the cash position, capital expenditure limits, and limits to size of tenders without needing to continually gain head office authority. Another control which works well is for the parent company to organise bonding so that if it does not approve of the subsidiary's activities it does not issue the bond. Nevertheless distance and time problems increase the risk that controls will be inadequate.

In the interviews there was considerable discussion of the merits of decentralisation and centralisation of decision-making and service functions. Both forms of structure have their supporters. The one common action taken in recent years was the enhanced central control of financial matters. Reasons given for centralisation generally include:

- the need to present an image of total capability to undertake a wide range of work requires bringing all parts of the organisation under one control;
- the same applied to the corporate image; whereas at one time some companies were prepared to have separate subsidiaries operating under their own name they are now being brought into the group image often under a new umbrella company;
- the need to have a strong central control particularly over finance; in some cases this control was always in place but the financial problems of the recession means that it is now rigorously enforced;
- cost saving by centralisation of accounting – quoted by one company.

Reasons given for decentralisation include:

- greater efficiency in devolving specialist functions e.g. personnel, training and safety, estimating, accounting, marketing and selling;
- more rapid decision making;
- saving of head office overheads;
- increased accountability for the business units;
- marketing advantages of retaining the identity of local subsidiaries.

Where it had been decided to reorganise a division or subsidiary in some cases the detail of the changes came from the top but in other cases detailed proposals were requested from the affected division; where the proposals were not radical enough they were 'sent back for rethinking'. Thus, both centralisation and decentralisation were seen by companies as a means of achieving economies in staff and overheads. The mere process of examination of current procedures may be enough to find ways of improving efficiency; the precise method of doing it is perhaps less important.

Where there has been decentralisation there has often also been a greater awareness at head office of policy functions as well as an enhanced advisory role and a greater focus on ensuring efficient cooperation between the units. In some companies where there has been decentralisation of certain functions, for example, of personnel there has also been centralisation of control in others such as accounting.

In order to reduce overheads the number of regional offices has been reduced in many companies especially the larger ones where some of them had about a dozen. In many cases because of the need to develop local contacts (see Chapter 5, Section 5.3.1) the larger regions have sub-offices. However the main functions of estimating, planning, accounting and personnel, where decentralised, are undertaken at the main regional office. Substantial overheads have been saved by this type of reorganisation. In one company the number of fully fledged regional offices was reduced from eight to four; in another from twelve to seven. But one company still has about seventeen regional UK offices each undertaking a high proportion of smallish contracts. Yet another company has actually increased the number of regional offices because it did not have adequate geographical coverage of the market.

A number of companies were keen that their regional offices should be run as autonomous organisations but at the same time were exercising strong control from the centre. There were some conflicts between these two approaches. One company had a director and a management board for each regional office which effectively ran the business but the main board laid down financial limits and approved strategy.

One company had developed some years ago a group manual dealing with all procedures from finance to employment. When this company acquires another business, which it has done on several occasions, it centralises all accounting and applies all of these procedures. Another company is initiating what it calls business process re-engineering, through which it is asking managers to question fundamentally the methods used in all aspects of the business. It hopes that this approach will involve more staff in seeking efficiency improvements. Although companies have slimmed down, on the whole they have not reduced the number of management layers.

Several contractors considered that the low profitability during the recession enabled certain actions to be taken which would otherwise have been very difficult. Much of the reorganisation and economies which were attributed to the recession needed to be implemented in any case but, because of the recession, they were more readily accepted by staff. It became possible to challenge beliefs about the way the business should be run. Managers reluctantly accepted sharing of secretaries, smaller cars and frozen salaries and in some cases cuts in salaries and part-time working. The crisis which faced all firms allowed admission of mistakes and problems to shareholders and employees and facilitated the acceptance of special provisions and write-down of asset values. The boom had fostered inefficiencies: it is very difficult to change a business for the better while that business is making money.

6.3   CORPORATE PLANNING

6.3.1   Planning from the 1970s

Corporate or strategic planning is the process through which firms can familiarise themselves with the implications of possible future opportunities, threats and other eventualities. Through this they can plan the future course of their business. Many approaches to corporate planning have been promulgated through management textbooks, executive development programmes and consultancies, especially in recent years.

Previous studies, in the 1970s and the 1980s,[3] have shown that one of the most significant features of those construction firms which were able to handle the effects of major recessions was the sophistication of their corporate planning systems. The 1970s recession saw the abandonment of formal corporate planning in many companies. An interest in the long-term future was replaced by a concern for short-term budgets.

An analysis of approaches to planning in the 1970s and the reasons for firms either maintaining or abandoning long-term planning highlighted two important issues. The first concerned the understanding which board members had of the objectives of corporate planning. The second was their understanding of the planning process.

In the first case those which abandoned the process believed that because the business environment was so uncertain it was impossible to plan. However, those which maintained their planning process claimed that it was exactly because the environment was uncertain that planning was required. They took the view that the process enabled them to familiarise themselves with uncertain but potentially threatening events, to think through the consequences of these and their possible reactions and generally to prepare themselves should these events transpire. This contrasted with the first group which saw planning as a process of delineating a path for the company into the future. Essentially they wanted planning to reduce uncertainty rather than to help them come to terms with it.

The second issue flows from the first. The planning process can be considered as comprising two phases. The first, the flexibility phase, is concerned with answering fundamental questions about the business of the firm and identifying possible alternative paths for development. The second phase, the efficiency phase, is concerned with deciding on which course of action to embark upon and then developing the most efficient way of travelling along this path. In periods of business stability firms do not have to spend much time considering flexibility issues; often sensible courses of action are easily determined. But they do have to spend a great deal of time on the detailed planning in order to achieve a high level of efficiency. In periods of business upheaval the situation is reversed. Being flexible and using the resources of a business in new ways is of paramount importance. Planning for efficiency without flexibility is useless.

Whilst the basic requirements of good planning have not changed, especially the need for relevant data, detailed market intelligence and a knowledge of those factors which influence a business and its environment, the 1980s saw an increasing importance being given to the need for a long-term vision of a business.

There is a similarity between the responses of firms in the recession of the early 1990s to that of the 1970s. In the 1990s those with less developed systems experienced greater difficulties in weathering the storm than those with more sophisticated systems.

The interviews also show that most firms reacted to the recession by giving less attention to their planning and by concentrating on a shorter time span and on the immediacy of severe financial and other problems.

The response of firms to the 1990s recession of abandoning their long-term planning processes and concentrating purely on short-term budgeting suggests that generally senior managers in the industry had little appreciation of the benefits of planning and had learnt little from the experiences of the 1970s recession.

6.3.2   The present position

The planning processes seem to have been of little real value when so many companies were seriously surprised by the recession and when, with its onset, planning was virtually abandoned. Now, it is creeping back into the lives of construction companies and they are beginning to look further ahead. There has been an increase in the number of companies which have adopted sophisticated planning. In the 1960s there were very few, in the 1980s rather more. Now in the 1990s the numbers have risen further.

Compared with the previous study managers are more able and willing to put forward and discuss business strategies. More companies are thinking strategically and some are actively engaged in and committed to strategic planning. In one company, the recently appointed

Chief Executive called on advisers from a financial institution to put together the detailed data which were lacking and were the essential pre-requisite to any drastic action and relied on a couple of management experts to work through the slimming mechanisms which were urgently called for. However, the horizon of some of these strategies is short-term and a few do not go beyond 18 months or two years. For example, in one company, a remedial strategy plan had been implemented with a horizon of 1993. This has now been replaced by another stretching to 1996. Whereas the former plan was intended to encompass all measures needed to overcome structural and financial problems the latter looks firmly ahead.

It was clear that the sophistication of the planning approach adopted by the companies varied greatly. Some felt the need for planning because of their general 'culture' of being analytical and risk averse. Others had learnt the lessons from needing to manage difficult situations whilst not having a planning system in place. Overall, although the planning process had improved in several companies only a third were regarded as doing it well.

There is no doubt that in the present environment companies have found planning difficult, if not irrelevant. All their efforts have been devoted to fire fighting in order to survive and only now are they beginning to think again of the future. They are very aware that they have to plan to be able to accommodate ups and downs and must become proactive.

Nevertheless in carrying out some of the interviews there was a feeling that some executives understood more about strategic planning than they admitted or perhaps appreciated. In some cases, despite being informal and possibly somewhat flawed in their outcomes, the approaches they adopted had similarities with those adopted in more structured approaches. Indeed there seemed to be some similarity between what one executive suggested as 'we think corporate strategy all of the time' and the admission of a site manager in another survey who claimed he thought 'critical path' even though he did not use the technique! There was a familiarity with the concepts, ideas and procedures but a cynicism, sometimes well founded, about their value.

With many companies having overstretched themselves by entering new businesses in the 1980s, many were pursuing very conservative strategies. However, even these did not reveal great sensitivity to changing market opportunities. For example, one operations director emphasised that the major plank of their strategy was to focus on 'doing what we do better' at a time when markets for their services were in flux.

In another company one of the main strands of its strategy is to concentrate on jobs of a few million pounds and below only on the grounds that this prevents the danger of one large contract going wrong which is always a risk.

Other companies offered some insight into the factors which underpinned their thinking about strategy. In one company for example, which is part of a large corporate group, four factors in particular were highlighted as essential to success: financial strength of the group and the confidence which it inspires, very high calibre chairman, the right philosophy, ie non-adversarial, and a quality training programme for its staff.

Perhaps the most telling comment about how one company was thinking about the future and reacting to the poor image and low morale in the industry was its quest to rediscover what was a basic tenet of the firm fifty years ago – 'that building should be a pleasurable experience for all involved'.

Some of the largest companies employed in-house specialists to provide background information as inputs to planning but by and large these assisted senior management in the development and compilation of long-term plans rather than taking the lead. The planning horizons were typically between three and five years, getting longer as the recession was perceived to be lifting. In most companies planning was characterised by a 'top down' and 'bottom up' approach. Top management provided overall goals and vision and divisional and regional managers identified opportunities and actions consistent with the plans of top management. Divisional management often worked within the scope of their businesses as defined by top management whereas top management had responsibility for ensuring that ideas for new businesses and other developments, wherever and however generated, if accepted, were consolidated and acted upon.

A few companies, largely the smaller ones in the survey, employed consultants to assist in developing their strategies. In some cases consultants were used purely as facilitators but in others they were intimately involved in putting the plans together. The companies which adopted this approach did so, firstly, because they could not and did not need to employ full-time planning specialists and, secondly,

because they found the approach of consultants more thought provok-
ing and dynamic than that of in-house specialists, who tended to be
'back room boys'.

6.3.3   Implementation of the plans

Two key features of the planning process are the way in which plans
are communicated to staff and how progress is monitored. Compared
with previous periods, corporate plans are now more often summarised
into much smaller documents and presented as a series of discrete business development projects to be undertaken over the life of the plan.
This approach helps the assimilation of the plans by staff throughout
the organisation. In some companies this entailed ensuring that all managers were aware of the plan by holding meetings with, in some cases,
100–200 staff. A few companies, however, are not so open with the
communication of their plans; only senior management know their contents. These are divulged to others on a need-to-know basis. This was
often a reflection of a belief in the need for secrecy but there was also
the view that middle management were not interested.

   One of the most frequent failings of corporate planning systems is
that they do not adequately address the implementation of the resulting
plans. Clearly if staff are not fully informed and made to realise the
significance of plans, implementation will be impaired. The approach
of presenting the plan as a series of business development projects
helps to overcome this by focusing on well defined outcomes, and on
the identity of those responsible for ensuring that these outcomes are
achieved. Provided that the projects are reviewed regularly, progress
can be monitored, deviations from the plan investigated and corrective
action taken. Clearly the projects are even more meaningful to those
who have to implement them if they have contributed to the planning
process and the identification of the projects.

   In one company, for example, planning commences with the divisions being asked to describe their vision and the objectives for their
businesses in five years time and the strategies they propose to achieve
them. These are then considered by the board, which meets for two or
three days. They examine how far the aggregated plan is likely to be
beneficial to the company, whether the resulting direction of the
company would be acceptable to shareholders, whether the group could

finance the proposed plans and whether there is a balance in the relationship of risk to reward. The plans then go back to the divisions for elaboration and amendment as necessary. Progress is reviewed every six months at meetings with the executive board and divisional managers. Short-term goals are selected and incorporated as business development projects. The company's planning documents used to be large and detailed but now they are much more manageable and of much greater practical value. One head of a division said he was happy with the company's plan because it was his plan!

In at least one other case a very major strategic change lies in the way in which the group treats the business plans of its divisions which is almost the opposite of that just described. 'Whereas previously the group accepted the figures from the businesses and summed them up to obtain the size of the group's desired financial cake now the group decides what size of cake it wants to bake and the businesses have to accept the size of their slices'!

Whilst it would be wrong to suggest that all companies were very sophisticated in their planning approaches there is no doubt that in many, managers are more aware of the plans than previously and more involved in their development.

References

1. Cadbury, Adrian, *Report of the Committee on the Financial Aspects of Corporate Governance* (London: Gee, 1992).
2. *Ibid.*
3. Lansley, Peter and Quince, Thelma, 'Organisational Responses to a Major Recession' *Construction Papers,* Vol. 1, No. 2, 1981, pp. 5–16. Hillebrandt, Patricia M. and Cannon, Jacqueline, *The Modern Construction Firm* (London: Macmillan, 1989).

7 The Management Resource

7.1 INTRODUCTION

The essential technologies of construction are embodied in the people employed and, unlike manufacturing, not in plant and machinery. Most construction plant is not project specific, it is interchangeable; it can be bought, sold, leased and hired. Exceptions may be found in work such as tunnelling where the equipment is specific to the activity. For most construction projects, however, it is not the equipment which is important but the way in which it is employed. Superior efficiency is not necessarily gained through using superior equipment but through using appropriate equipment in a superior manner, as a result of good selection, planning and management. Whether in the design office or on the construction site, it is the way in which the hard technology is managed which influences project success.

Whilst it is common-place for chief executives to claim that the crucial resource of a firm is its staff, it might also be argued that over the last few years individual members of staff have also become more like items of plant – acquired, contracted, disposed of and retired. Thus the paradox of the recession has been that whilst everybody still acknowledges the importance of people and of managers to the construction industry, by their actions they have also implied the lack of importance of the individual, except for very special members of staff. This is reflected in attitudes towards graduate recruitment and the neglect of management development and training.

During the boom the industry rapidly expanded the number of its managers and professional staff. In many cases expansion was into new and exciting areas, which required novel approaches to working with clients and to the organisation of complex projects. The boom created a new style of manager in the construction industry, an upwardly-mobile cohort of graduates better able to relate to clients' needs than previous generations. Professional practices and project management consultancies working with mainly blue chip clients and high profile property developers offered well paid interesting employment. Few contractors could match these attractions but those that did also developed quite different 'sub-cultures' in those parts of their companies which followed the new ways of doing business.

During the mid-1980s contractors became aware of the need to improve their image and to increase graduate recruitment. In the early years building and development companies had suffered from the cutbacks imposed on universities. Indeed, in the early 1980s without support by the industry itself a number of degree courses were closed down. The 1986 Lighthill Report[1] on degree and diploma courses was followed by many initiatives by the industry and individual firms to improve the flow of young able people into construction and to retain them. Senior management became much more involved with training and recruitment issues. Industry sponsored degree courses, continuing professional development (CPD), in-company training, even custom made MBAs became *de-rigueur* to the personnel and training executives who increasingly populated the industry. As a result the image and attractiveness of construction degrees and careers improved and the number of graduates increased although it still remained difficult to recruit students of the right calibre to construction degree courses largely due to the continued poor perception of the industry. Nevertheless, the job market for new graduates was excellent, and for those with a few years experience even better.

Despite these changes, within many contracting firms management development activities were quite modest. There was a conflict between the need for good managers and the intention to train for the future. Often staff were regarded as too valuable managing projects to be spared, although there was a concern for their development and progression. Nevertheless they did gain a great deal from managing projects at a busy and exciting time.

This chapter reports on some of the changes taking place in the employment of managers in the industry in the wake of the recession. The next section (7.2) considers problems arising from reductions in staff and necessary cost cutting. It is followed by a section on changes in construction employment patterns. The issues of the recruitment and development of managers are dealt with in Sections 7.4 and 7.5 respectively.

7.2   PROBLEMS OF STAFF SHRINKAGE AND COST CUTTING

In the companies interviewed the number of managers had shrunk dramatically in the period since 1989 by from 10% in some firms to over

30% in others. In 1994 several companies predicted more redundancies to come. The heavy reductions in staff were due to the shrinkage of the workload and to the urgent need to cut all costs, including overhead costs. The cuts seem to have taken place right across the range of activities and types of employees.

Some companies regard the statutory redundancy provisions as poor, especially as they have not been increased recently, and these give staff enhanced redundancy terms – in some cases about double the statutory requirement. This represents a high cost to the company. Early retirement at 55 or 60 instead of 65 years of age is another way of reducing staff. If the company has a well funded pension scheme this is not too difficult but such generous schemes are usually limited to the directors and senior staff. However whether it is early retirement or redundancy, as one person put it 'there is no nice way of telling a man he is losing his job'. Some companies were concerned about the future of their redundant staff and felt guilty about the way they had let some of the employees down. Several directors made comments such as: 'in the late 1980s we asked young men to join the industry, we enticed them with good salaries and promises of long-term careers and then we sacked them in their thousands'.

Many companies have tried to find alternative employment for their redundant workers. One company set up counselling and support services and arranged a redeployment fund. But many individuals had great problems accepting the reality of redundancy and did not want to take totally different types of jobs. For some head office personnel work sharing and reduced salaries were less painful alternatives to redundancy.

It is not surprising that the morale in most companies was at a very low ebb in the early 1990s, especially in those which had made large staff cuts but also those where financial problems made clients suspicious of their viability. Staff were always 'looking over their shoulder'. Some said 'the poor image of the company was damaging morale'. This depression amongst staff was worsened by other cost-cutting operations including freezes or even cuts in salaries. In addition, in boom conditions many staff had been earning substantial bonuses which have since disappeared. Some employees had share options which had lost much of their value as company shares plummeted. A more visible sign of bad times was the down-grading of company cars. The results of the cuts were very apparent with more stress, illness, worry and a loss of sense of humour. This traumatic experience of the recession is likely to have a permanent effect on employment conditions and on the attitude of employees.

On the other hand the fact that the whole industry was suffering and the clear necessity for attacking the whole range of costs enabled companies to take measures which in normal times would have lost them staff and would have caused enormous resentment. On the whole people buckled down and got on with their jobs remarkably well.

Several companies said that the redundancies they had been forced to make in the early stages were not too damaging to their businesses because they got rid of the least satisfactory managers–often those appointed at a time of acute manpower shortages whom they would not have employed had the choice been wider. Then came further redundancies when good people had to go. If staff had to be reduced further they would need to deplete key personnel who were perceived as vital for the continued long-term health of the company.

At the same time as some companies lost their least satisfactory managers, in other cases good managers left for other pastures because they were worried about the continued health – even the continued existence, of their employers. Other companies saw this as an opportunity to strengthen their management and to fill gaps which had developed. Thus a number of companies now claim to have stronger management, but most are weaker.

Finally, however, there was little support for the view that the recession had made managers more effective. Many were working too hard, in the hope of avoiding redundancy. Much of the intrinsic satisfaction of working in the industry, traditionally higher for managers in construction than in other industries, has been soured.

7.3   CHANGE IN CONSTRUCTION EMPLOYMENT PATTERNS

Before the recession there was already much mobility amongst top managers. They often moved from their original company, in some cases to return at a later stage. Headhunting had become prevalent in the boom years.

Nevertheless most companies still prefer to grow most of their senior managers and it was a matter of regret to some that they had recently had to recruit from outside. Indeed they saw this as a failure of their policies on progression planning. However even within the companies which like to have home-grown managers, the merits of recruiting some with experience elsewhere was acknowledged. In others it was regarded as acceptable to fill about a third of the vacancies from outside. In one company the policy was simply to get the best person for the job. Nevertheless some felt it necessary to monitor the perform-ance of newcomers very carefully to make sure that they 'fitted in' or, in terms of the terminology prevalent in the 1980s, that they adapted to the 'culture' of the company.

At the other extreme some firms recruited from outside to obtain insight and acumen for a well established part of a business, and in others outsiders had been recruited with the intention of changing the orientation and image of the firm as well as its future direction.

The impact of a major change in its top management on the construc-tion division of one firm was dramatic and moved it from a very tradition-al building firm to one which was amongst the leading 'market makers'. That a traditional firm had been able to achieve this says much for the success of its recruitment policy and for the flexibility of traditional staff who had to accept many changes. However they could see the benefits of a new regime which generated work and, thus, limited redundancies.

All firms need some permanent staff to manage sites but in the current environment vacancies tend to be filled with staff employed on contracts for the duration of particular projects. There is more accept-ance of agency-recruited personnel in spite of the high outgoings because, in the long run, the avoidance of redundancy payments and other costs means that short-term flexible employment is cheaper. This would have been unthinkable by many of the contractors interviewed in the middle 1980s. Then they were afraid that new managers would be unable quickly to integrate into the company and its 'culture' – a more important concept then than now. When the industry gets onto an even keel again, it may be that the acceptability in some companies of short-term employment of managers will decrease but they currently see the policy being maintained for some time to come.

Some chief executives described successful top managers largely in terms of being entrepreneurial individuals who sought opportunities, identified and exploited them, did deals and ran projects. They were generally thought to have distinctive personalities with a ruthless streak. However in a number of cases managers who had been able to cope with the boom conditions were found lacking in the skills required in the recession. They could not efficiently manage businesses that had been allowed to develop in an uncontrolled way and were now out of balance with market conditions. During the recession managers had to be prepared to dismiss people and to take unpopular decisions. In some companies it was necessary to appoint outsiders to achieve restructuring and to slim parts of the business. Such individuals were not necessarily required for long-run management and, having fulfilled their roles eventually left their companies. In some companies, however, it is feared that those who ably managed the cut-backs may not be able to manage a stable state nor the renewed growth of the business.

Although there are still very good opportunities for technically orientated managers the professional background required of top managers is now less important than general competence and ability. Lawyers, bankers, accountants and financial analysts hold top positions in several companies. This was not the case ten years ago, especially at main board level. In contracting a construction background remains very important and it is possible for a contracting manager to move to a non-contracting business but the opposite is more difficult.

There are two views about specialisation versus breadth of managers. Some say that because contracting divisions are becoming more specialised in their work, they need more specialised managers. There has been, in at least one company, less reliance on generalists compared with functional specialist managers. One consequence is that the transfer of managers between divisions has become more difficult. However the contrary point has been made by some, that the manager in charge of a division needs to be more flexible than in the past. He has to display multi-disciplinary qualities and be able to cross boundaries between types of work and functions. This is a reflection of the change in the environment in which contractors operate.

This greater flexibility has always been important for overseas work where there are no back-up services and where managers have much more responsibility for running projects and developing future work. The switch to working overseas seems to present fewer problems than in the 1980s. In part this is because the communications systems and methods of control have greatly improved and also because some contractors have given more independence in the UK to their site and contracts managers who are therefore used to being in total charge of a major project when they go abroad.

There are differences of opinion as to whether civil engineers can move to building or vice versa. In some companies it is not unusual for a civil engineer to manage a building contract but others say they have not got the mind for the detail of building and are not as cost-conscious as builders. Most companies would not put a builder in charge of a civil engineering site because of lack of technical knowledge but others say that for some simpler types of work, for example small bridges or service stations, it is possible to make this switch. This whole issue has become very important as civil engineering workloads have not been affected by the recession to the same extent as building so that the potential for staff transfers is important. Moreover in spite of the considerable increase in civil engineering work in the past decade, the number of qualified civil engineers is much greater than is required by the amount of civil engineering work available and, in spite of the recession, some firms have experienced a shortage of good quality graduate builders.

There is concern that the UK contracting industry has less able, less well qualified staff than the French and the German industries. In these countries the elitism of the best educational institutions attracts high calibre students into engineering and construction and gives them a first class, broadly based, education. Those in joint ventures with European contractors are experiencing this at first hand. They are impressed with the quality of their counterparts, though they have also observed that UK managers have greater financial and legal skills and tend to be more adept at solving management and commercial problems.

7.4 GRADUATE RECRUITMENT AND MANAGEMENT TRAINING

Graduate recruitment and management training have suffered because of the decline in construction activity. Sandwich degree courses which rely on students being placed in industry for one year during their four year programme have had to be dramatically reshaped, with serious consequences for the education of the students. Despite their best intentions, many firms have not been able to maintain their support for increased graduate entry levels. Whilst some have maintained sponsorship of degree courses, graduate recruitment, graduate sponsorship and training programmes, these are the exception. Upon graduation the prospects for employment in the industry have been bleak. Exacerbated by an over-supply of courses in building and surveying, graduate unemployment has become a serious issue.

The boom period saw significant developments in the availability of higher education to those in the industry, for example, through open and distance learning and part-time degree and higher degree courses. Some companies recognised the value of such courses, were supportive and encouraged independent study. In the recession, however, the staff became concerned that the time and effort involved in personal study might be regarded as a lack of commitment to their job.

Generally, as a result of the recession, the training function of most firms shrank. Training budgets and training staff decreased and in-company training and management development programmes were seriously curtailed in all but a few firms. Whilst some firms have kept faith with those special initiatives which they supported during the boom, they now cannot guarantee employment to the students they sponsor and provide little formal development for those whom they do employ.

The responsibility for training, or at least its cost, is increasingly devolved to operating units. Many central training departments have to cover their costs through the operation of an internal market for their courses. There are inevitable problems and conflicts of interest. Some operating units lack expertise in identifying training needs and in understanding what is available. Others are tempted to save money by not paying for the training of staff who might move to another operating unit.

Despite these comments some firms have maintained their training activities and even increased the range of training opportunities. Some training departments have mounted more courses than ever, even though the number of participants has been less than in the boom period. In many cases the courses have been trainee or graduate trainee oriented or have had a strong technical orientation, often linked to legislation such as Health and Safety. Courses in financial appreciation and control, presentational skills, report writing, project planning and marketing were frequently mentioned in the interviews. Those which offer a more integrated and strategic appreciation of business and which groom staff for senior management roles are rare.

At top management level some firms tend to rely on the once-in-a-lifetime attendance of staff on a management development course at some prestigious institution (for example, London Business School, Harvard Business School, INSEAD). A number of companies also employ a mixture of consultants or facilitators to identify management needs and to help tease out future strategies. The latter can play a very significant role, especially where firms lack comprehensive corporate development and strategic intelligence functions. Their functions were no doubt already available from consultants at the time of the earlier study but they were regarded simply as a type of management consultant. Some top managements, however, have been reluctant to engage such experts for advice. This was either because they thought there was no merit in such advice, because they were well resourced internally or because they felt that outsiders did not understand their business.

7.5 DEVELOPING MANAGERS FOR THE FUTURE

It is sometimes argued that construction firms are players in the market and that, as market traders, they act as brokers for opportunities and resources and not as developers of either. If this is so it is inevitable that the construction firm will have difficulties in planning its resources and developing its staff. Thus to expect a firm to invest heavily in staff development would be absurd, given the nature of the market and the strength of the competition. Indeed this does appear to be the case. Many of the companies visited spoke of difficulties in developing and even retaining staff. They spoke of their failure to plan adequately for management progression, even for those positions where the need was obvious, and to appreciate the changing nature of the skills which they required. Whilst many attempted to adhere to a policy of promotion from within and to place tried and trusted staff in key positions, quite often they were forced to recruit from outside, because either the internal staff they originally had in mind were not good enough or had been attracted elsewhere.

In many cases the most obvious failing was in providing high flyers with a good insight into areas of business strategy at an early enough stage in their careers, and in ensuring that they had received a good grounding in inter-personal skills, team building and decision making. Because management development programmes are unusual in construction firms, there was a great concern for every course to be a success, and not to disappoint or upset participants or their senior managers. As a result training programmes appeared to be rather ordinary and low risk. Often they followed the pattern of courses established in the mainstream of management development some years before. There is a clear need for courses which raise awareness of issues and discuss a range of solutions as a part of a planned management development programme.

Chief executives were concerned that whilst training, development and succession planning were very necessary, they did not automatically produce the top management material – the bright sparks – which the firm needed. There seemed to be a conflict between the beliefs of some chief executives about the characteristics of top managers and those which could be engendered by formal personnel and development policies. In part this might be reflected in the relatively low status of the personnel and training functions and more generally of human resource development in a number of construction firms. The essential stimulus to the development of managers comes from being in a thriving growing business. It can be complemented by a well judged training and development programme and, possibly by the greater involvement of individuals in future planning.

Some companies have formal manpower plans and these may be reviewed annually with identification of key people, their successors, the gaps and hence the needs. The planning in one company originates with middle management in the operating units and then moves steadily through the organisation up to the main board. In another the process starts at a higher level and goes down the organisation. Many companies however acknowledged that their manpower planning was not good enough and that they should pay more attention to it. This is somewhat surprising in view of the emphasis placed by companies on contracting being a people business.

Ultimately, it is the chief executive who has responsibility for the long-term development of the business and hence of its management. Where senior executives are committed to management development the implementation of a policy can work well, with the personnel manager having an advisory and coordinating function. It would appear that only personnel managers are in a position to keep abreast of best practice and its application in the areas of recruitment, assessment, appraisal, training and staff promotion development programmes, besides the vital knowledge of legal aspects of employment.

It is in the introduction of appraisal schemes where personnel managers have taken the lead. Views about the effectiveness of the schemes vary but no more than in other sectors of industry. Their development and implementation require a great deal of effort and commitment from top management. These have been forthcoming in some of the companies which in turn had been reasonably satisfied with the schemes. However, the recession, with its attendant uncertainties about long-term employment, career progression and training needs has hampered the operation of the schemes.

Since the previous study the status and nature of the personnel function within construction companies has not improved. The role of most personnel managers is limited. Except for the few individuals who by their personal characteristics have raised their status and influence, the personnel manager is seen as an administrator of policies determined elsewhere and not as a policy maker.

Reference

1. Lighthill, J., *Degrees in Building Management: Demand, Provision and Promotion* (London: BEC/CIOB, 1986).

8 Review of the Survey

8.1 INTRODUCTION

This chapter considers three broad questions. First, how key areas of strategies of firms differ from those described in *The Modern Construction Firm*[1] for which interviews were conducted mostly in 1986. This was at a time when the industry had experienced rising output for five years. Output continued to rise to 1990 from whence it fell to 1993. Secondly it compares in broad terms the results of this survey with another on the effects of recession on construction and with one on the effects on UK quoted companies. Thirdly it considers the question of whether the firms are fitter and leaner to cope with the demands to be put upon them or whether they are weaker and thinner and will be unable to respond effectively to future changes in the level or structure of demand.

8.2 CHANGES IN STRATEGY 1986–1993

8.2.1 Key developments in strategy

The major changes in strategy from 1986 to 1993 have been as follows:

- concentration on core businesses;
- greater focus on balance sheet matters compared with profits and cash flow and greater financial sensitivity;
- greater attention to marketing as an important business tool;
- correcting the neglect of international markets;
- tightening of structure and organisation of companies;
- continuation of policy of reducing permanent employment even covering managerial staff and shrinking of training and support for education.

A much broader study by Geroski and Gregg[2] of the reaction to recession of a sample of some 600 large UK quoted companies classifies the responses into three groups – financial decisions, strategic decisions and cost control. Table 8.1 shows some results and also gives

Table 8.1   Responses to the recession: UK industry and construction industry

		UK industry* %	Construction[†]
a)	**Financial Decisions**		
	Disposal of Assets	52	virtually all
	Reduce Dividend Cover	35	?
	Introduce a Rights Issue	14	about half
	Reschedule Debt	23	?
	Increase Short-term Borrowing	35	?
b)	**Strategic Decisions**		
	Focus on Core Businesses	83	all
	Increase prices	42	0
	Change Marketing Strategies	70	all
	Merge with/Acquire another Company	23	0
	Rationalise Product Lines	50	na
	Develop Overseas Markets	52	half
c)	**Cost Control**		
	Close Establishments	56	few
	Reduce Employment	83	all
	Reduce Employee Wage Growth	85	all
	Reduce Inventories	65	na
	Scrap Outdated Machinery	31	na
	Reduce Headquarters' Costs	72	all
	Contract out Auxiliary Services	34	no change

Notes: '?' not available
'na' not applicable
Source: *Geroski, P.A. and Gregg, P., 'Coping with the Recession', *National Institute Economic Review*, November 1993, pp. 64–75; and [†]the interviews.

some comparable data for construction companies interviewed in this study. These results indicate actions judged to be of some importance or very important to a company's response to the recession.

The first part of the table highlights how all large construction companies in the survey were forced into disposing of assets whilst a large percentage of them had to raise funds through rights issues in order to reduce borrowings. Major strategic decisions were taken by all companies, notably focusing on core businesses and changing their marketing strategies. Most of the companies operating abroad have tried to increase their activities. Though one or two companies took over other companies, this activity was small and did not approach what is described as merger. Their pricing mechanism, based on tender, dictated reductions in prices as otherwise they would have obtained little work. Rationalising production lines in an industry where each product is unique was obviously an option not available to them.

Cost control was vital. All contractors in turn reduced employment and in many cases paid lower salaries and wages, especially if bonuses are taken into account. They also cut back on head office costs and rationalized regional offices but few of them were actually closed. Here too, reductions in inventories and scrapping outdated machinery were not available options. Some further tabulation of their responses is shown in chapters 3 and 4.

8.2.2   Corporate objectives

In 1986 the principal objectives of firms were growth and diversification. In 1993 they were to develop core businesses and restore profitability. In 1986 firms saw the benefits of a buoyant market in the following terms:

- an increase in cash flow from contracting operations;
- an increase in profits;
- the ability to fund additional investments in other types of business;
- a broader field of operations nationally and internationally;
- the ability to deal with very large projects;
- impressing clients with their capability;
- an increase in their range of activities in order to spread risk;
- satisfaction of personal ambitions and aspirations.

In so far as they have survived in the form in which they were operating in 1986 all of the companies, with one exception, grew from 1986 to the peak of the boom. They grew partly by organic growth and partly by acquisition. The latter was often a major step in their diversification activities and at the time virtually all of them put this as one of their objectives. There were five groups of reasons for diversification:

- the implementation of a growth policy;
- the wish to increase efficiency by, for example, controlling the source of supply of materials, or taking over subcontractors in order to have control over a broader range of operations;
- the utilisation of the cash generated by contracting in more profitable but more cash hungry businesses and the consequential increase in fixed assets, which was beneficial to Stock Exchange valuations;
- the desire to spread risk by being involved in businesses with cycles, risks, and client dependencies which did not coincide with those in the construction sector;
- the personal interest of individual board members in some other business or the purchase of a different type of business as part of some other acquisition objective–almost acquisition by accident.

Throughout the 1980s companies did diversify for these reasons, often into construction-related businesses such as housing, property, minerals, equipment, specialist subcontracting services. Where they were already in these markets, they moved into specific niche areas within them. They also diversified into non-construction activities including mining, waste management, and leisure.

The doleful saga of the reduction in the size and profits of the businesses as a result of the recession is told in the main body of this book. This reduction included the sale of many businesses, most of which were subsidiary to the main activities of the companies, but some of which they would have preferred to retain. This has ensured a greater concentration of specialised activities and a focus on core businesses. The profits of the core business of contracting fell during the recession but on the whole did not disappear. Contractors now realise the need to concentrate their activities on businesses where they have special expertise. What they regard as their special expertise varies from company to company but generally includes contracting and often housebuilding, property and minerals.

Generally contractors still seek growth, partly because they are, at the present time, smaller than previously, but also because they aim to remain or become large national or international contractors and they see the need to be larger to compete with the large European contractors. Size is still important as they need to be big in order to be awarded large contracts. Thus growth remains an objective, but to a lesser extent, tempered by a realization that the UK market is unlikely to return to its peak for some time, and that overseas markets are very competitive and crowded by other companies. Also, companies have been frightened by the consequences of over-expansion in the late 1980s. They are hoping for growth in the overall market not so much to enable them to increase in turnover but to reduce the level of competition so that prices and hence profits improve. Greater profitability is a much higher priority than growth in turnover.

Many of the reasons for diversification in the 1980s are no longer seen as relevant. Most companies said that diversification is not something they seek as a means to growth. Contractors do not see the need for control over a wide range of site-related activities as they did in the 1980s. This is partly because there are no longer shortages of materials or subcontracting services. The main contractor is thus able to obtain whatever is needed in terms of quantity, quality and price without having to own the supplying organisation.

Financial reasons for diversification have also disappeared. In the 1980s contractors were assuming that a large positive cash flow was going to continue indefinitely and they were therefore willing and able to invest in fixed and hence permanent assets. They now realize that they are simply holding clients' and suppliers' funds. They have seen the cash available shrink with a reduction of turnover. In the late 1980s they invested too much in cash-hungry businesses which turned out to be unsustainable in the 1990s. Firms also need higher fixed assets for the satisfaction of the stock market but this is dealt with later Section 8.2.3.

The reason for diversification which is still seen as very important by a few companies is to spread risk by being in more than one business, preferably contra-cyclical ones. This policy includes geographical expansion, into for example, South East Asia, the Middle East, North America and Australasia.

There is a new reason for diversification, which was not apparent in 1986, namely to obtain contracts which include both the construction and the operation of the facility. This is described in Chapter 5. Examples are the operation and management of such diverse businesses as railways, prisons, hospitals, roads and bridges, almost always with an expert partner. Companies often take equity in a project rather than operate on a fee basis. However, the equity has the same objective as in conventional property development projects, that is, to guarantee that the contractor will get the work. Another way of obtaining work is to be involved with the setting up of projects involving finance, feasibility, and design. Again this is a form of diversification.

After the traumas of the period 1989 to 1993, at the beginning of 1994 construction companies were starting to consider anew their longer term future. Although some directors spoke of their companies having a vision, few offered a meaningful integrated view of their future which could have served to motivate and commit staff to the firm, to the attainment of that vision and hence the enhancement of their careers. However some directors proposed significant developments to their businesses within the medium term.

The companies had varying long-term objectives but there were some common themes which may be grouped under growth, profitability, markets and portfolio. These included:

Growth

- to become a major force in the construction industry or a dominant player
- to grow in the core businesses
- to increase turnover
- to have larger and profitable regional offices
- to remain one of the largest companies in the UK
- to achieve progressive growth
- to achieve moderate growth to restore shareholders' position
- to refrain from seeking turnover for its own sake

Profitability

- to earn profits consistently
- to outperform the industry average
- to be in more high value added businesses
- to increase efficiency
- to have profitable regional offices

Markets

- to increase amount of work abroad
- to broaden engineering base
- to become involved in financing infrastructure projects
- to change the mix of work

- to reduce dependence on UK markets
- to move into building products businesses when industry picks up

Portfolio

- to concentrate on the core business
- to balance cash generating and cash consuming businesses
- to maximise position in existing markets before taking any further new ventures
- to maintain a number of local businesses
- to keep a core business in housing without a large land bank
- to balance risks and profits in housing and contracting
- to avoid speculative property involvement
- to balance international and UK businesses
- to maintain in-house expertise in property

Not all objectives applied to every company and the smaller of them in particular did not generally put growth high on their objectives, if at all. Nevertheless growth has returned as an important issue and many companies are considering acquisitions as a means of expansion. The merits are that growth by acquisition is quicker than internal growth. One company put its maximum growth rate at 15% per annum without stretching the infrastructure of the business too far. One or two big projects can achieve this. If on the other hand a business is bought, for example in civil engineering, then a track record is inherited and growth is instant, say, to double the previous level. One director said about a possible acquisition 'we would heave a sigh of relief and stop thinking about poaching managers to achieve organic growth'.

Whereas at one time it was fashionable to look for contra-cyclical markets, most companies are now looking at markets where growth is expected and withdrawing from declining ones. There are still, however, some companies which lay emphasis in their long-term thinking on operating in contra-cyclical markets. This is one of the attractions of various mineral businesses, such as coal which have markets outside construction.

Some also felt that having a portfolio of several construction related businesses was still a valid approach even though the recession had created serious difficulties. Contracting, housing and property development could be made to hang together effectively provided that firms recognised the inevitability of significant fluctuations. The error in the past has been the expectation of a steady overall pattern of activity and misjudging the length of the current recession.

8.2.3 Financial policy

Financial policies have had to be restructured and redirected to limit the damage caused by over expansion, falling asset values, excess borrowing, low profits and falling cash flow. Companies have been dealing with one crisis after another, often on a daily basis. The first stage of dealing with this situation has generally been completed and they have been able to reduce their gearing to acceptable levels.

The 1986 objective of finding outlets for positive cash flow was rather too successful in the late 1980s because the cash-hungry businesses absorbed more cash than was available from the contractors. Cash flow is strictly available for a very short term. Companies' investment of cash flow in long-term assets was not prudent. They were assuming that cash flow would continue at past levels and that it would be available in the long term in spite of its transitory nature. In the recession contractors had to sell cash-hungry businesses and were still left with very high gearing.

Another way of dealing with the problem of high gearing resulting from borrowing in a boom period was to obtain more money from shareholders by rights issues. At the same time companies were cutting costs, especially overheads, controlling very carefully all items of expenditure and making very good use of any cash which was available.

The main objective is now increasing profitability. Whilst this has always been a company objective, today it is imperative for survival. There is a tendency for firms and observers to breathe a sigh of relief and claim that the crisis is over. For many the immediate crisis is over but the remaining problems are considerable. Companies have to produce a reasonable return on share capital which, with rights issues and other share issues, is made more difficult than before. Moreover the return on the increased share capital has to be achieved having sold off, or ceased to trade in, some of the more profitable businesses which enabled healthy returns in the past. The reduction in opportunities does not help companies. They have been able to reduce overheads substantially, but there is still not enough work available for an industry in which there are too many companies chasing too few contracts.

8.2.4 Markets and marketing

The markets in which contractors operate have changed since 1986. From 1986 to 1989 construction companies were increasing their involvement in property development, housing and other diversified businesses as well as contracting. Then came the recession and the return to the core businesses discussed in Chapter 4. By 1993 most, but not all, companies had withdrawn from or were still trying to extricate themselves from property holdings and at least one had also withdrawn from housing development. Many of the peripheral activities have been sold. However, one or two have recently moved into housing.

In 1986, it was commented in the *Modern Construction Firm*,[3] 'in general the contractors interviewed are prepared to undertake any type of building or civil engineering work' (p. 21). This remains the case, contractors are desperate for work and will take on almost anything though some are not involved in civil engineering:

- the large contractors undertake much smaller projects and are competing with medium sized contractors. This is because the number of large projects in the UK has dwindled and the total work available has fallen between 1990 and 1993 by 9%;
- they actively seek very large projects through joint ventures;
- several companies, which in 1986 had run down their overseas work and then permitted it to fall further with the boom in the UK, look to expanding abroad again.

The greater changes have however taken place in product differentiation. In 1986 four distinct ways of differentiating the product were identified:

- by offering a range of different ways of managing the project;
- by the extension of the construction phase backwards into design;
- by the extension of the traditional project backwards ahead of the construction phase to include putting together a financial package;
- by the forward extension to include equipping and furnishing the building, maintenance of the building or structure and the management of the facility.

At that time the first two were undertaken by most companies but by separate business units and some contractors were just beginning to develop competence in the last two. The first one, of providing for the client whatever type of contractual arrangements he required, is now common practice; the second, design and build, is prevalent and the last two are becoming increasingly important. One new development is the provision of equity capital for individual projects by the contractor as a means of obtaining work. Another is that contractors are trying to go even further back in the development process and identifying projects which the potential client had not himself considered (see 5.4.2).

The first two have become integrated into the main contracting businesses. The third involves investment of substantial financial resources. The last requires completely new skills and attitudes. These methods of product differentiation require a very proactive marketing policy and the changed marketing approach for these types of operation has also affected the marketing stance for more traditional types of project. Chapter 5 outlines the response of contractors to the fall in their workload and illustrates that they are no longer willing to wait until they are invited to go on a tender list. Indeed without marketing themselves they would be out of business. Marketing has arrived in the construction industry.

8.2.5　Structure, organisation and management

During the recession serious deficiencies were revealed in the structure and organisation of companies including:

- main boards which were too large;
- inadequate control of operating units;
- inadequate control of finances, especially borrowing and cash flow;
- inadequate cooperation between parts of the company;
- overmanning in senior management.

In 1986 nearly all these deficiencies were identified as dangers in comments by the authors or by some of those interviewed. to quote from the previous study, *The Modern Construction Firm*:[4]

'There appears to be a conflict between the desire to ensure that the constituent parts of the company are represented on the board and the recognition that its efficient functioning requires its membership to be limited' (authors' comment, p. 95).

'When the expansion geographically and into other activities took place, with the subdivision of the group into more operating units,

the control and monitoring processes were not increased *pari passu.*
At the same time the changes in the environment and in group policies mean that more monitoring and control and more sophistication
may be necessary' (quote from contractor, pp. 97–8).

'The impression gained, however, was that ... a number of them
have not yet established a fully relevant set of financial criteria and
systems' (authors' comment, p. 55)

'One of the main objectives of the restructuring is to ensure that the
various operating divisions of the building company learn from each
others' experience in all areas of the business instead of operating in
watertight compartments' (quote from contractor, p. 98).

There is evidence from many companies that the ease with which
profits were generated permitted very lax management control. It was
not until the recession that firms took action to rectify these problems.

To some degree all of these areas seem to have been tackled. For
example the size of main boards has reduced from a norm of 10–13 in
1986 to the present norm of 6–8. Management and financial controls
have been strengthened substantially. Some companies have reduced
the number of operating units especially regional offices – partly to
reduce overheads but also for control reasons.

Although the standard of planning is still not very good, overall in
the companies visited in both surveys it seems that improvements have
been made in about a third, a half appear to be unchanged and a few
have probably got worse. Where they have improved this has often
been in terms of a better relationship between the appreciation of
opportunities by top management and the implementation of resulting
plans by those responsible for operations. Another improvement has
been the translation of the overall plans into short-term objectives for
each unit and the monitoring of the achievement of these objectives.
Planning has also improved in determining choice of markets in which
to operate.

During the late 1980s companies increased the sophistication of their
management systems; for example, many introduced formal appraisal
systems and enhanced their training programmes. Graduate recruitment
became the norm and there was a general concern for the development
of managerial and professional staff resources. With the onset of recession most of these developments were reduced or abandoned.

Manpower planning became short-term as companies reduced staff. Management training almost ceased in some companies. Graduate recruitment virtually stopped. At the same time there was a change in attitudes to long-term employment. Many site staff recruited in the late 1980s were dismissed as projects were completed unless they were part of the core management team. Companies are much more likely to use agency and 'contract' staff , whereas in 1986 this was regarded as exceedingly unsatisfactory because it was claimed that such staff would be unfamiliar with the company's 'culture' and its methods of operating. As a result of the recession, the quality of managers in construction firms may in some cases be better than in the past. A few, however, may now be short of good managers who moved to other companies to safeguard their careers.

8.3   LEANER AND FITTER OR THINNER AND WEAKER?

There is a well established school of thought that recessions are beneficial because they create a period in which companies are forced to re-examine what they are doing and improve their operations, sometimes colourfully called the 'pit stop' theory.

The key indicators of efficiency in the functioning of construction companies are mainly in the following areas which are discussed below with respect to the period 1989 to 1993:

- control of the main board;
- supply of efficient managers;
- efficiency and sensitivity of planning;
- scope of marketing;
- financial strength.

The initial stages of the recession revealed great weaknesses in the control of company operations by the main board and senior management. Since then companies have shrunk their boards and their membership is more directly relevant to the operations of the whole business; non-executive directors are more focused, old retainers have gone, and main board members have been chosen for their ability to take an overall view of the business as well as for advice on specific non-operational aspects of the business. Of the companies assessed it was revealed that from the beginning of the recession to the end of

1993 control by the board had improved in at least half of the companies. It had remained the same in the remainder.

Although there was seen to be a definite improvement in the quality of management at board level there was little clear improvement in the quality of management in general. One company had a policy of employing head-hunters to recruit high quality senior staff. Another had a policy of enhancing its management through training and development. A more general feature was that firms in slimming down had been able to get rid of weaker management. In perhaps a quarter of the firms interviewed the quality of management was thought to have improved. In over half of the firms there appears to have been little change. In less than a quarter there had been a significant fall in quality, particularly because these companies had lost their way and good staff were leaving as well as being dismissed.

Should it be necessary to shrink any further, firms will lose very good people and their ability to expand their operations effectively and quickly will be severely impaired. Neglect of training and low recruitment levels will have adverse implications for their efficiency in the medium term.

They have been essentially preoccupied with short-term issues of keeping afloat rather than looking to the longer term. They still do not understand the benefits of planning in terms of identifying alternative courses of action to meet the uncertainty of the business environment. The fact that some aspects of planning have improved should not conceal the fact that there are still serious deficiencies in planning. Some major construction companies probably still compare badly with leading firms in other industries, especially those which are capital intensive where investment decisions require a long-term view.

The recession and the dearth of work has forced companies to identify new or better ways of selling their services and products. This has involved a more detailed examination of potential markets and to some extent the creation of market opportunities. It is judged that about half of the contractors interviewed had improved their marketing between 1989 and the end of 1993 and in only one or two had marketing faltered. Companies have a more sophisticated approach to marketing but there is still some way to go in making this activity more effective.

The crisis which hit most contractors at the beginning of the recession has, to a large extent, been dealt with. They have reduced their excessive borrowing by the sale of assets, cost cutting and financial restructuring including rights issues. However the finances of a number of companies remain precarious. Profits are low and there is little immediate prospect of substantial improvement. Furthermore companies no longer direct, neither do the banks permit, the use of cash flow for longer term business developments. However, the advantages of a positive cash flow are substantial.

Nearly half of the firms interviewed in both studies were considered to be in a weaker financial state than previously and others, though stronger, suffered from low profitability and were vulnerable. A number of companies have increased share capital on which dividends will have to be paid when they return to a reasonable level of profits. In addition, although bankers have reluctantly continued to lend to them in the hope of salvaging previous loans, in the future it will be much more difficult for contractors to convince them that they should lend money for new developments.

The recession has forced some improvement in management in the top companies especially in control by the board of the operations of the group, in planning and in marketing. However, it has been quite disastrous in its consequences for the financial health of the companies. It has forced financial reorganisations which have been damaging for many and in particular has forced the sale of certain assets which would have been better retained by the companies. Unless the level of profits can be substantially improved further crises will arise and any further cut back in the level of activities of the firms will prevent satisfactory responses to future rises in demand. Because of the improvement in management large contracting firms could probably grow by, say, 10% of turnover in real terms in the first year of any recovery without serious reductions in efficiency and at a slower rate thereafter. Any one firm might be able to grow in the short-term at a faster rate. Previous work[5] found that a long-term growth rate for individual firms of 10% a year was feasible. However there is a limit to what an individual firm can do to overcome the problems forced upon it by the state of the industry and the economy.

The construction firms are leaner and fitter in management terms but thinner and weaker, indeed very weak in financial terms. Firms are vulnerable; the viability of some is still at stake. Unless their financial situation improves their management will also deteriorate.

References

1. Hillebrandt, Patricia M. and Cannon, Jacqueline, *The Modern Construction Firm* (London: Macmillan, 1990).
2. Geroski, P.A, and Gregg, P., 'Coping with the Recession', *National Institute Economic Review*, November 1993, pp. 64–75.
3. Hillebrandt and Cannon, *op. cit.*
4. *Ibid.*
5. Lansley, P., and Quince, T., 'Organisational Responses to a Major Recession', *Construction Papers,* Vol. 1, No. 2, 1981, pp. 5–16.

Part III
Practical and Theoretical Implications

9 Contractors' Concerns for the Future of the Industry

9.1 OVERCAPACITY

A major concern of all the contractors interviewed was the excess capacity in the industry especially amongst the larger firms. Excess capacity, as they interpret it, means that the number of firms competing has reduced less than the number and size of projects. The fact that the employment of managers has shrunk in many companies by as much as the workload is less relevant because it does not affect the level of competition. The effect of increased competition for projects is a drastic fall in tender prices and low or negative profits from contracting.

There are several reasons why the capacity of the industry has fallen little among the largest firms:

- positive cash flow enables funds to be pushed around to where they are most needed and prevents low or negative profits which create a situation in which the company cannot pay its bills;
- banks have been prepared to continue to lend money to profitless companies because if they refused such support they would lose their previous loans;
- investors have been similarly prepared to subscribe to rights issues because they would otherwise lose any chance of a recovery in the value of their existing shares.

In the circumstances it is difficult to see in what way the capacity could be reduced. However, several ideas have been mooted and these are discussed here.

The first is the question as to whether there should be mergers of UK companies. The benefits to the firms concerned of merging are very small or even negative. Savings from mergers are basically confined to the reduction of the head offices and some regional offices. Moreover the chance of one merged company winning a contract is the same as either of the companies separately. Lastly where companies have merged in the past the results have not been good. Each company has

139

tried to protect its own staff, identity and image resulting in few economies and sometimes disastrous management.

A second possibility is takeover of the weaker company by the stronger one. This is more likely to happen than merger on an equal basis. The savings could be greater because the dominant company would not be prevented from slimming down the acquired company as long as it was not contrary to the TUPE legislation. The other benefits to the purchaser are dubious unless it is buying specific know-how, work in progress or some other asset which it cannot otherwise acquire. However now that the gearing of most companies has been substantially reduced, the weak company can limp on for a long time in the hope of an improvement in its situation.

Only if there are several mergers or takeovers would there be a significant impact on the capacity of the industry. However, the companies which merge would not benefit much more than others in the industry. The incentive to merge is, therefore, small.

A view has been canvassed that concerted action by the banks could enforce mergers of construction companies which might improve the safety of loans.

Another matter raised was possible mergers with or takeovers by European contractors.

This was thought unlikely on any scale because:

- the price/earnings (PE) ratios of contracting companies are unattractive;
- foreign shareholders do not like the more open stock market in the UK;
- the construction environment in the UK is more competitive than in some other European countries.

On the whole mergers seem unlikely as company collapses permit a reduction in capacity and survivor companies are able to acquire any work in progress or recruit skilled staff at a much lower cost than via a merger and have some choice as to work in progress or staff they wish to take-on.

Another consideration is whether the capacity at the top of the industry could be reduced by a reduction in positive cash flow. Some continuing clients are reported to be scrutinising bids and rejecting those with front loading. Furthermore bonding reduces cash flow. However builders merchants' credit and delays in payments to subcontractors until after the monthly certificate payment is received are unlikely to cease. The process of reducing capacity through reduced cash flow would take too long.

A possible solution lies in the need to fund the initial stages of projects and to finance major projects. The practice of contractors taking equity in major projects is gaining ground as is the move worldwide towards greater private participation in infrastructure investment. In addition, the capital invested in simply obtaining the project, often with a very long gestation period and heavy design costs, means that contractors need more funds. Their availability could become critically important because without the necessary capital funds at its disposal a contractor would not be able to obtain large contracts. This is a very different situation from that in the past, when contractors could operate with very low capital and, at all levels, the industry was characterised by ease of entry. Increased requirements of capital for bonding also create a type of entry fee and help to limit tenderers, as might a tighter regulatory framework of accreditation for tendering opportunities, registration of operations and firms and quality requirements such as BS5750.

Large capital requirements to obtain major contracts could produce an elite group of large contractors distinguished from others by their greater capital resources, a form of premier league. Successful companies would be able to raise capital in the market and thus join the top ranks. Those companies which could not raise capital would be relegated to smaller contracts. They would either do less complex work but remain large or shrink to medium size companies. One consequence might be the demise of family-controlled companies in the top rank, because they might need to dilute their shareholdings to raise funds and so cease to be family controlled. One way out of this would be for the family to hold the majority of voting shares. It is possible to have some of the equity in non-voting shares but as these are disliked by the financial institutions it is difficult for firms with non-voting shares to raise substantial amounts of capital.

There is, thus, no ready answer to the question of how to reduce capacity.

9.2 OPERATIVE EMPLOYMENT

The practice of labour-only subcontracting which is well embedded in the industry has been reinforced by the recession which imposed heavy cut-backs in manpower in the industry. Most contractors see no possibility of its reversal. At one time labour-only subcontracting was much more pronounced in the South than in the North but the latter also now uses mainly labour-only and specialist trades subcontracting with a decreasing amount of direct employment. Though those firms which have a strong base in the North still have more substantial direct employment, the only directly employed are key personnel, including foremen. In general the smaller of the large firms also seem to have a larger proportion of direct labour than the very large ones. The firms which still have directly employed operatives say that they do not wish to place themselves in the hands of subcontractors and that it is easier to motivate direct labour. They also point out that for the industry not to employ its own labour is bad for training, for safety, for continuity of employment and for quality of work. There are also some signs that there may be difficulties ahead for contractors with labour-only and self-employed labour.

First, the Department of Social Security can insist on payment of National Insurance contributions and can even claim back contributions if a person is working for only one employer. Secondly, the Inland Revenue is getting more strict about the award of 714 certificates which enable main contractors to pay subcontractors without deducting tax and national insurance contributions. Thirdly the construction trade unions are campaigning for new laws to overcome some of the disadvantages of self-employment. UCATT no longer battles against labour-only but is actively recruiting the self-employed and needs to be seen to be acting on their behalf. In fact self-employment is a preferred way of life for many during a boom but in a recession the lack of benefits make it much less attractive.

Together with pressures exerted by the DSS and Inland Revenue directives, new employment protection laws could remove some of the flexibility and induce at least a partial swing back to directly employed labour. This would be welcomed by some contractors since it would facilitate training and improve safety standards. It would also create problems because direct employment needs more supervision than labour-only paid on a piece-work basis.

At the end of 1993 very little operative training was undertaken by contractors. One company which in 1989 took twenty trainees now takes two. They do not have work on which to train them and in any case it is uneconomic to do so. Some companies have negotiated with subcontractors to provide some practical training.

Two companies undertake training on behalf of the industry under the auspices of CITB and local Training and Enterprise Councils (TECs) and Local Enterprise Councils (LECs). Because of the local involvement, the training contractor has to deal with up to 30 local training monitoring organisations depending on how many centres are run, and these audit the training. One contractor complained that in fact these organisations 'audit everything except quality'. Also, funding has been reduced; whereas payment was formerly made in advance, now it is in arrears.Whilst the National Vocational Qualifications (NVQ) which are being administered by these centres were described as 'quite good', the administration of the paper work involved was seen as very costly. There is little or no money to be made from these training schemes but the contractors involved at least can make an informed selection of persons to recruit. Finally, one company also does some training in developing countries, for example, Sri Lanka, under the aegis of United Nations Organisations and ILO, but again it found it difficult to cover UK overheads.

One contractor not involved in training or certification welcomed the NVQ system because employment of well qualified operatives would help to overcome the poor image of the industry. The company thought that labour was not paid enough and partly blamed this for the low standard of entrants to the industry. However many in the industry are confused by NVQs especially by their relationship to highly regarded qualifications such as City and Guilds Certificates, ONC and HND.

Several contractors stressed that the supply of trained operative labour was vital to the industry. They are concerned at the uncertainty over the future of CITB which makes it very difficult for it to function effectively. Properly funded organisations for operative and supervisor training are absolutely necessary and 'unless some alternative is established the demise of CITB would be a disaster'.

The reduction in the labour force brought about by the recession, together with the long-term reduction in training by the industry means that, if and when there is an upturn in work, there is unlikely to be sufficient trained manpower.

9.3   POLICY AND REGULATORY FRAMEWORK

The two previous sections dealt with concerns of contractors which are specific to the construction industry. Those interviewed also expressed

anxieties about processes of government and the regulations of the
European Union which directly or indirectly affect the well-being of
the industry. They fall into two broad groups: the implementation of
financial policies and the regulatory framework.

While most contractors recognise that the management of the
economy overrides any concern by government for individual industries, they nevertheless consider that the government could have
demonstrated greater understanding of the problems faced by the construction industry in the past few years. A major concern focuses on the
lack of appreciation by government of the importance of timely decisions in a market situation. Associated with this is the industry's lack of
a strong voice with government during the depths of the recession, if
not for a longer period. Delays in the approval of projects either for
financial or planning reasons are damaging to the efficiency of the
industry because of uncertainties in workload and high costs in retaining teams which could complete the work. Delays in payment are especially damaging since they directly affect cash flow. The unacceptably
long duration of any discussions, negotiations or enquiries before innovative ideas can be implemented is damaging not only to the industry
but to society at large. This procrastination by government is widely
condemned by contractors. An example is the attempt to involve
private funding in public infrastructure projects which have been pro-
moted by the industry and the financial institutions and welcomed in
principle by government for a number of years but have not yet led to
any generally acceptable regulatory formula for proceeding on a broad
front. The problem seems to be that government does not realise that if
private financiers are taking risks they must have commensurate profits.
If a satisfactory framework could be developed the principle of private
finance for public sector projects could cascade down to much smaller
projects. More generally, contractors complained about the 'dead hand'
and short-termism of the Treasury. Even when proposed schemes could
reduce the level of public expenditure by introducing more private
finance, public bureaucracy and regulation prevented timely developments with an adverse impact on the welfare of society.

Although there was general support for the impact of the Single
Market and especially for the award of regional and social funds to less
well endowed areas, contractors were critical of some aspects of
European Union regulations. On the one hand contractors complained

about what they considered as the excess of regulations introduced in the past few years by the European Union and, on the other hand, the slackness of the monitoring mechanism to ensure their effective implementation by individual members of the Union. In particular there was felt not to be a level playing field in the implementation of the Public Procurement Directive.

A major enquiry into the affairs of the construction industry has been undertaken by Sir Michael Latham[1] on behalf of the government and industry (see Section 1.2). The aim was to recommend ways of improving the performance of the industry by suggesting ways of overcoming many of the impediments to efficiency and effectiveness which although acknowledged for many years have seen little progress towards their resolution. There is a need for simpler and more consistent contractual arrangements, streamlined tender procedures, better co-ordination of project information, sensitive handling of financial payments, incentives for innovation and improved performance, better client representation to the industry and better industry representation to government, the government to play the role of a model client and a host of other requirements, many of which have been touched on in this report.

Curiously most of those interviewed were circumspect about the Latham Enquiry. 'So many previous enquiries have gathered dust on the shelves'. Although the issues dealt with by the Latham enquiry are important, in the struggle for survival individual companies were prepared to go to almost any length to secure work and to exploit the opportunities which presented themselves. The recommendations in the Latham report required an attitude towards business relationships which was viewed as not consistent with those engendered by the business environment in which most companies and individuals have to operate. Latham's recommendations that there should be a Standing Strategic Group of the Construction Industry chaired by the Secretary of State for the Environment or other DoE minister and an implementation forum of industry leaders, could result in some progress. This will be the case, however, only if there is a determined and concerted long-term campaign from government, industry and clients. Since the campaign will need to extend for much longer than the periods of service of most government ministers and those senior spokesmen for the industry who are in positions of influence it is difficult to envisage how momentum will be maintained.

Reference

1. Latham, M., *Constructing the Team* (London: HMSO, 1994).

10 Towards the Redevelopment of Theory

10.1 INTRODUCTION

The first book in this series: *The Management of Construction Firms: Aspects of Theory,*[1] offered a number of theoretical approaches from different disciplines which help to analyse and explain the decision-making processes in large construction companies. The second book: *The Modern Construction Firm*[2] examined the way companies behaved in the mid 1980s – a period of the early stage of the boom, a time of great optimism, growth and expansion. It considered also the relevance of theory to the actual behaviour of companies. Having examined the situation during and after a major recession in the industry, it is appropriate to look again at theory to see how relevant it is both in boom and slump and how progress may be made in developing a better understanding of the basic principles underlying the industry's operations.

In *The Modern Construction Firm* it was concluded that some of the theory was not relevant to the organisation, structure and behaviour of construction companies (pp. 159–61). This latest study identifies another problem, namely that much of the theory is relevant to a period of stability and growth but much is irrelevant in a period of crisis and decline in the industry. This is particularly evident in relation to business objectives and strategy but also in other areas.

In this chapter some of the theoretical approaches outlined in the first book are considered in the light of first, selected developments of theory which have taken place since then and secondly, results from the 1986 investigations and the present studies. This chapter selects those aspects of theory which are most relevant. The matters discussed are treated in a variety of ways in the previous two books and in earlier chapters of this one. Appendix 2 lists the main chapters which are relevant to the subheadings of this chapter and also reproduces the list of contents of the first two books for easy reference. The book entitled *The Management of Construction Firms: Aspects of Theory* is referred

147

to as the Theory Book and *The Modern Construction Firm* as the
Industry Book.

10.2   STRATEGY

There has been a change in approaches to strategy in the last decade so
that strategy formulation is regarded as the role of the entrepreneurs in
a company and planning and planners have been distanced from the
creation of new ideas for the development of the company. Strategy
formation is regarded by many writers[3] as a process with inputs which
include a considerable amount of intuition, an ability to synthesise
ideas and information from a number of different sources and the utilisation of analysis. Planners can provide analysis, record the strategic
objectives and then plan the more detailed implementation. It seems
that in the construction industry there was always that distinction
although it may have become more apparent in recent years. Corporate
planning is discussed in Section 10.4.

According to Ramsay[4] in the Theory Book in the chapter 'Business
Objectives and Strategy', the first consideration in defining strategy is
to determine the scope of the business, the second is to identify the distinctive competence of the business from which flows the allocation of
resources, the third thread of strategy is to specify the competitive
advantages of the firm and the last is to consider whether there is
synergy between various parts of the business.

It was found in the survey, undertaken in a period of upswing, and
reported in the Industry Book, that the principles underlying strategy
formulation were accepted though not necessarily implemented.
Various aids to identifying the appropriate markets utilising the ideas in
the theory are discussed in Ramsay. They are further considered in
Section 10.3.

The work of Porter[5] on competitive advantage and the means to
achieve it is discussed by Ramsay and is still a much-used guide in this
area. Ramsay quotes Porter who finds two main ways to obtain market
advantage over competitors, by cost leadership or by product differentiation. Porter also has another way which is a mixture of these two, that is,
to enter a niche market either by cost advantage or differentiation. The
construction industry has cut its costs quite drastically in the last few
years and no doubt, at least while there is a shortage of work, will strive

to lower them further. Companies are however differentiating their product and creating niche markets as is shown in Chapters 4 and 5.

The ideas put forward by Ramsay were regarded as very relevant and in the Industry Book it was concluded that 'Ideas in Ramsay's Chapter should be widely disseminated' (p. 160). It is clear that these ideas were developed against the background of growth and expansion for firms in any industry. The discussion is about the rate of overall market growth, not the rate of market decline and the assumption is that the firm has a choice of what markets it will be in, based on its internal strengths and the state of those markets. In the early 1990s many markets have been in decline and strategy formulation has focused on survival by types of action not described or contemplated in Ramsay's analysis.

The objectives of companies during the recession changed from growth to survival and that implied concentration on financial matters such as reducing borrowing and limiting losses. The time span of objectives in many cases became weeks or months rather than years. Normal objectives and long-term strategies were put into cold storage.

There has been little work in the last few decades on the effects of recession on company behaviour. However, a few theorists have looked at the effects of recession and decline and discussed their implications for theory. Of particular relevance to the current situation is work by Stuart Slatter[6] who in 1978 studied companies in the UK which had turned around their business from decline to recovery. In studying forty such companies, of which thirty recovered and ten failed, he found that asset reduction and new methods of financing were used for almost all successful turnaround companies. Divestment was the most common cash-generation strategy. Improved financial control systems were important. He found however that the major difference between those firms which recovered and those which failed was 'the quality of implementation' of their measures. These results were not very different from the conclusions of the present survey (see Chapter 3).

Another contribution comes from Kathryn Rudie Harrigan[7] who looked at strategies for firms in declining markets. Although it is not suggested that the construction industry is in permanent long-term decline, though some of its product markets may be, her findings about 'end game' strategies for firms in industries which have passed their halcyon days tend to be confirmed by this study. In particular her work raises issues about the extent to which firms analyse competitive behaviour within their markets rather than work to past experience, their understanding of the expectations of clients and the threat from alternatives (for example IT).

Generally, much of the theory on strategy, especially that on markets (see below), is not relevant to a period of recession without very considerable adjustment.

Almost all companies in this second survey said they wanted to retreat to their core businesses. The businesses they defined as core are listed in Section 4.2 in Chapter 4. What are the characteristics of these businesses? They are generally those businesses which have some or all of the following characteristics:

- the company has been in business a long time and therefore has expertise;
- a fairly substantial turnover;
- it is either profitable or expected to be so in the future;
- it expects reasonable market growth or has a captive market;
- it has low capital requirements.

Some of the businesses not regarded as core would have been so regarded in a previous period but one or more of their characteristics had lost relevance and the businesses were no longer in favour. On the other hand some would have remained in favour but were disposed of because they were saleable, largely because they were profitable and could be presented as distinct self contained businesses, such disposals saved many of the companies in the study.

10.3 MARKET PORTFOLIOS

An example of how much the theories put forward in the 1980s assumed growth in markets is reflected in the Boston Matrix as described by Ramsay[8] in the Theory Book. Figure 10.1 below shows in the top two sections the Boston Matrix as originally used and the bottom section is an extension to show market decline. The vertical axis shows market growth per annum and in the bottom third, as extended, market decline. The horizontal axis shows relative competitive position. The circles represent businesses, their size proportionate to turnover. The businesses could be broad ones in construction such as contracting, property, housing, and mineral production as well as waste management and a whole host of smaller businesses.

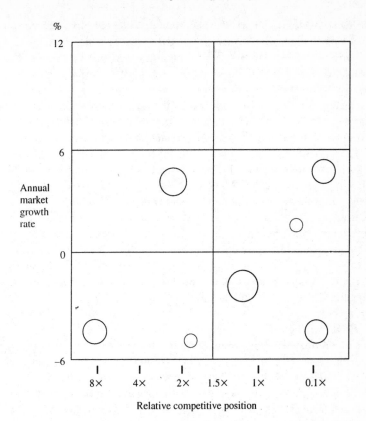

Figure 10.1 Extended growth-share portfolio matrix
Note: Size of circles indicates turnover. Relative competitive position is mea-
sured by ratio of turnover of company to that of leading competitor.
Source: Based on Figure 2.2 in Ramsay, William, 'Business Objectives and
Strategy' in Hillebrandt, Patricia M. and Cannon, Jacqueline, *The Management
of Construction Firms: Aspects of Theory* (London: Macmillan, 1989), the
Boston Matrix, extended and amended as described.

   In the Boston Matrix the top two quadrants are normally regarded as
beneficial, and particularly the top right quadrant because there is great
market growth and a chance to increase market share, and the bottom
quadrants are regarded as less desirable. The underlying assumption of

the Boston Matrix is that all businesses are potentially profitable. In a declining market, which is usually linked to low profitability, large size of turnover, as shown in size of circle, may well be undesirable. The problem is that in the business environment of the 1990s recession a high relative competitive position was often a bad thing, not a good thing, because profitability was negative so the larger the market share and turnover, the more money a company would be losing, that is given the assumption of potential losses being spread evenly across all projects!

In fact market share in construction is relatively unimportant because for almost all companies it is very small not only in contracting but also in other businesses. Market growth is very important because it determines the level of competition and hence profitability.

Ramsay, in any case, makes it clear that this approach is too simplistic (p. 16) and then goes on to describe the General Electric and McKinsey model[9] reproduced below as Figure 10.2. Here market prospects are on the horizontal axis and the business strengths on the vertical. Though reversed in location they are similar to market growth and competitive position but are vaguer and therefore open to broader interpretation.

However the businesses being disposed of in the recession were often not those with low profitability in which the business strengths of the company were low, as would have been expected by the matrix in Figure 10.2, but those relatively high on both counts. This is because those low on the rating were unsaleable or would produce practically no cash from the sale, so that companies which needed to realise large amounts of cash were forced to sell the wrong businesses.

Thus Figure 10.2 – the General Electric and McKinsey model – remains valid in the long run. It identifies the businesses to be disposed of, including some with low profitability, and those which should be developed. However in crisis the model has to be set aside.

What then is the justification for the use of the model in a crisis situation in which cash must be realised for survival – in this case to pay off loans and to reduce gearing? What mattered in the decision to keep or sell were market values determined by, for example, profitability and market prospects and the scope of the business envisaged by companies especially in view of the general retreat from peripheral businesses (see below). A practical matrix is illustrated in Figure 10.3. In this figure profitability is on the vertical axis and the rating of the business from core to peripheral on the horizontal axis.

	High	Medium	Low
High	Investment and growth	Selective growth	Selectivity
Medium	Selective growth	Selectivity	Harvest/ divest
Low	Selectivity	Harvest/ divest	Harvest/ divest

Business Strengths (vertical axis)

Market Prospects – Industry Attractiveness (horizontal axis: High, Medium, Low)

Figure 10.2 Industry attractiveness and business strengths matrix
Source: Ramsay, William, 'Business Objectives and Strategy' in Hillebrandt, Patricia M. and Cannon, Jacqueline, *The Management of Construction Firms: Aspects of Theory* (London: Macmillan, 1989), table 2.3, page 17.

If a business A, peripheral to the main operation, was very profitable it could have a high market value. The same business would have a low market value if profits fell and perhaps a negative value if it was making losses. Businesses B and C differ from A in that they are nearer to the core the firms want to keep. There would be other businesses with higher market values than A, B or C, even though profitability was lower, just because of their size eg D. During the recession contractors were forced to sell businesses with high market values. They would

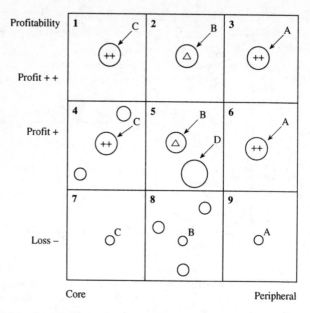

Figure 10.3 Profitability – business type matrix
Note: Size of circles indicates market value. Pluses indicate businesses with positive cash flow and triangles cash hungry businesses.

have started with those peripheral to their activities but were in some cases forced to move to the middle area and sell businesses which they would have preferred to retain. There is another consideration of great importance in construction businesses namely whether they have a positive cash flow as opposed to being cash hungry. A business with a high positive cash flow might have been retained even though it had a lower market value or was more peripheral than another business which was cash hungry. Since contracting has a high positive cash flow and was the core business of all but one of the companies visited and was important to the remaining company there were two reasons for retaining it. This is indicated in the figure by pluses for positive cash flow and triangles for cash hungry businesses. Business B might well have been disposed of in preference to business A because it is cash hungry in spite of being nearer to the core activities.

Relative competitive position or market share is not very important compared with profitability and in various contracting markets as opposed to varieties of construction markets such as property and housing, even less so because there is fairly easy transfer from one market to another. Market growth rate is however important. One might therefore have a diagram as in Figure 10.4 below on which to base

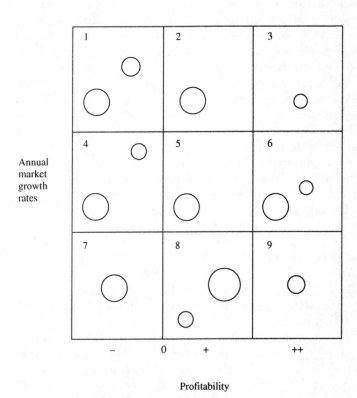

Profitability

Figure 10.4 Growth–profitability matrix
Note: Size of circles indicates total turnover.

long-term non-crisis decisions about the businesses to be in. This figure plots them according to expected market growth rates and profitability.

A company might have a small niche market with a high market growth rate in area 3 or at the other extreme an unprofitable business with a low market growth rate in area 7. In fact it could have a whole range of types of minor specialisms and expertise areas probably spread over the whole of the matrix. It would withdraw from those which were unprofitable with low market growth but would probably strive to improve profitability for say a largish business in area 1.

The ways in which profitability can be improved in all types of businesses are basically to reduce costs or to increase prices. In contracting, except by particular differentiation of product, say, through better marketing and by gaining economies of scale, if they exist, by increasing volume by lowering prices (see Chapter 5), it has to be done by reducing costs. Or, if by increasing prices, then, because of the tendering system, the implication is a reduction in success rate and therefore in volume of work if other factors remain the same. However, other factors do not remain the same and high market growth will often enable contractors to raise prices without reducing volume and therefore to move from area 1 to area 2. In the recession with low or negative market growth this was rarely possible so that contractors had to concentrate on reducing costs by lowering overheads, including cutting back support staff, stopping training, closing down offices, etc. and freezing salaries, cutting down on company cars and other employee benefits.

10.4   CORPORATE PLANNING

One possible definition of corporate planning is the means of achieving objectives and strategies and that is the way Ramsay[10] approaches it in the Theory Book.

In the section above some of the matrices have been discussed and adjusted for the special characteristics of construction and for a market in recession as well as a growth market. Some analysis of markets in matrix form is very important to understanding existing businesses and to projecting forward various possibilities. Such understanding is a prerequisite for planning. However these tools are useful only when a firm has some idea of where it wants to go and the motivation and determination to take action.

In contracting, Ramsay distinguishes between the consideration of what the markets are and how they may develop and where the individual firm's competitive advantages lie. Ramsay cites the process of construction with four phases: conceptual, design, contract documentation and construction on site as the key to a contractor's market development leading to a successful business. In the traditional process the contractor has the conditions imposed on him but he needs to set down the conditions preferred by himself. In 1986 the contractor's marketing was focused mainly on exploiting growth markets and getting on tender lists (see the Industry Book, p. 63). Markets were defined first in terms of end product and secondly geographical location, the latter being more important for international work. In the boom contractors were keen to participate in development by having an equity stake and when the market turned down major clients took the lead in requiring contractors to supply different services including some provision of finance. The collapse of the commercial and housebuilding markets forced contractors to focus much more on their own competitive advantages and also on different ways of offering their services.

They began to do what Ramsay suggested they should do which is 'to take the process apart and put it together again...'. In fact the contractors were not the originators of this approach. It began with the major clients and was adopted by contractors. Ramsay did not anticipate this because he looked upon most clients as quite unsophisticated.

In the last decade or so attention has been given to several writers who have questioned the value of the formal approach to strategy as proposed. In particular, James Brian Quinn, a member of the so-called 'incrementalists', maintains in *Strategies for Change – Logical Incrementalism*[11] that the formal systems unduly emphasise 'measurable quantitative forces at the expense of the qualitative, organisational and power-behavioural factors that so often determine strategic success'. He views strategy as developed by a series of sub-systems within the organisation, with each sub-system taking into account the attempts to learn about an essentially unknowable future. It is the function of the central management to reconcile sub-system strategies with each other to produce an integrated enterprise strategy. This is not muddling through but adopting a proactive and purposeful practice to achieve ends.

More recently Mintzberg[12] in *The Rise and Fall of Strategic Planning* stresses that strategy and planning are quite different. He regards strategy as something developed and synthesised in the mind of the entrepreneur while the role of the planner is to codify and make explicit the strategy and then to programme or plan so that it can be implemented.

Stacey[13] also questions the validity of conventional theories and tries to reconcile the opportunistic approach, so often adopted in practice, with conventional strategic management. He dismisses the notion of some grand strategic plan and because of the uncertainties inherent in any business, and particularly construction, he recommends a flexible, step by step, process of business development based on experience. He stresses that companies should not be trapped by a grand design but be able to change or even reverse policies in keeping with what is actually happening in the outside world. Stacey's orientation has merit as long as it is linked to an overall long-term view of what the business should be like and good intelligence as to the trends and developments in the market.

These last approaches have a different emphasis to that of Ramsay in the Theory Book but he too regards planning as a means of achieving objectives and strategies.

The authors of this book have always advocated a flexible approach as is apparent in Chapter 6 and this is what large construction companies generally do. In fact they made attempts to do what is now regarded as formal planning beginning in the late 1950s and early 1960s but the hard numerical method applied to everything was soon changed to a more flexible method of planning. Those in the industry who do plan fairly well do so more in line with the Mintzberg approach than according to the more formalised approach to planning. In particular,

- they formulate overall strategy at the top based on a mixture of intuition and informed analysis,
- they ask the operating units to present their plans to the board so that they can be incorporated into a consolidated plan,
- they use planning departments to provide background information and analysis and to develop the board's deliberations into an operating plan,
- they build into the planning process means of changing their strategy in the light of changed external and internal circumstances or their own change of mind.

Nevertheless, although there has been a great deal of research and development in the formulation of approaches to developing corporate strategies and the work of for example Porter and Mintzberg has attracted a great deal of attention from consultants, trainers and planning specialists, construction firms have developed their own methods rather than following the prescriptions and advice of the planning gurus. In the 1980s some firms were very attracted to the approaches to corporate development popularised by books such as *In Search of Excellence* by Tom Peters and Robert Waterman[14] and its sequels. This was largely because they recognised the entrepreneurial, irrational even cerebral elements in developing a business which had been so ignored by previous generations of writers and by the business schools. Notions such as vision, action, culture and loose-tight systems were recognisable by the construction executive especially when presented in the refreshingly attractive manner of Tom Peters.

Some companies virtually abandoned planning during the recession but one could argue that that too was an aspect of flexibility because their objective became survival and measures to achieve this were required immediately.

There are a number of ways of implementing the planning process. Important factors are that the plan should be a working document known to all those required to implement it and it should be developed by a top-down approach, led by senior management, and bottom-up approach led by the operating units. The techniques of planning are described in many texts, of particular relevance to construction are those by Langford and Male[15] in *Strategic Management in Construction* and Stacey[16] in *Dynamic Strategic Management for the 1990s*.

10.5 DIVERSIFICATION

In the Theory Book the advantages and disadvantages of diversification were discussed in the chapter on diversification by Cannon and Hillebrandt.[17]

The theory of diversification identifies horizontal diversification in which firms expand into different unrelated activities and vertical integration in which they move into the businesses of their suppliers or customers. Several elements of the theory of diversification are of particular relevance to contracting. The first is the need to spread risk by overcoming fluctuations in workload, controlling essential supplies and in ensuring markets. The second is to make better use of resources, mainly skilled personnel and cash since contracting is not a capital intensive activity.

There have been a number of reasons for a change of attitude to diversification and these call for some readjustment of the theoretical guidelines.

First, companies which diversified horizontally to obtain some protection from cyclical fluctuations have often not found such protection. There are several reasons for this failing. The most obvious one is that the businesses were not contra-cyclical or that the recession was so deep that even those which should have behaved less like construction suffered severe dips. Disappointments in this respect included, to some extent, property and housing as well as a miscellaneous collection of small businesses. Another reason why firms have not found protection in contra-cyclical businesses is that such businesses have to be quite separate from construction and this usually implies that management expertise in the new businesses is lacking in construction companies with the result that performance is below expectations. Lastly non-construction businesses are often capital intensive and, whereas in the boom construction companies had money to invest, in the recession they were short of capital and could not find the funds adequately to maintain these businesses. Thus although the reduction of risk is still a valid reason for horizontal diversification, it is a very difficult one to pursue. In many cases it is replacing a risk of fluctuation with a risk of failure in a business which may also be subject to fluctuation and which is insufficiently understood.

Secondly companies had diversified to gain control over their sources of supply or their markets, that is, they had diversified vertically. Reasons for wanting control over supplies in the mid 1980s included inadequate quality of supply; price rises due to shortages and actual shortages of supplies at the right time and place. In the recession a buyers' market replaced the power of the suppliers and it was no longer necessary to own sources of supply in order to guarantee appropriate supplies. Moreover the lower demand for these same supplies meant that some of the businesses acquired for vertical integration were not even profitable. The advantage of vertical integration and hence diversification especially backwards still stands from a theoretical point of view but it should carry a 'health warning' – 'Potentially dangerous during a period of recession'.

A third major reason for diversification in construction was to find a use for cash surplus to requirements and this reason is more or less specific to the construction industry. However the construction companies burnt their fingers badly because they were using funds which were, in reality, clients' property and only temporarily in their hands, to undertake long-term investments in property, land and other assets. This was regarded as acceptable because, while turnover was maintained or rising these funds were continuously available. However as soon as turnover fell they were no longer available in the same quantity and companies were forced to borrow. This type of diversification should, with hindsight, be deleted from the theoretically sound reasons for diversification. However, there remain many valid reasons for diversification, for example, acquiring or developing an asset base in other sectors using retained earnings rather than short-term cash surpluses.

10.6   INTERNATIONAL CONTRACTING

Seymour's[18] exposition of the theory of international contracting stands up to scrutiny in the light of developments in boom and recession. The three conclusions bearing directly on the action of individual companies are first, that an overall strategy on overseas operations is of vital importance and it should be based on differentiation of products in overseas markets. Unfortunately many companies during the boom neglected overseas markets because they had so much work in the UK but they are now regretting that they did not retain their level of involvement and are trying to rectify the situation. They are basing their marketing on differentiation of products. The second point, that ownership advantages, that is, assets of expatriate contractors not available to local contractors, must be relevant to the region where the firm chooses to operate, is also valid. There was a burst of enthusiasm about operating in Europe in the late 1980s and early 1990s, which has to some extent petered out. A reason may well be that the ownership advantages available to UK contractors are also available to local European contractors so that the second criterion is not satisfied. Lastly Seymour concluded that 'more use should be made of joint ventures and consortia of contractors in developed countries'. The advantages of joint ventures and consortia is that they spread the risk over a greater number of companies and increase domestic competition by enabling smaller companies to join together with foreign partners. A third advantage is complementarity and synergy where the whole is greater than the sum of the parts.

10.7   FINANCIAL STRATEGY

In the Theory Book the chapter by Cannon and Hillebrandt on 'Theories of the Firm'[19] considers the theoretical justification for profit maximisation and the Industry Book, with the results of the survey, found that increasing pre-tax profits was an overriding financial objective. During the boom companies over-borrowed and invested immensely. During the downturn in construction activity almost all firms shifted the emphasis of their strategy to dealing with balance sheet problems including reducing gearing by sale of assets and obtaining other finance. Now that the worst of their balance sheet problems is over, they are again focusing on increasing profits as their main objective.

Much of the chapter on finance by Cannon and Hillebrandt[20] in the Theory Book is of general applicability and holds true in boom and recession. At the end of the chapter consequences of the special financial features of contracting are discussed. The most important ones are identified as positive cash flow and minimal requirements for solid assets.

In both the previous two books great stress was laid on the importance of positive cash flow which enabled contracting businesses to expand with limited dependence on external finance and in some cases provided finance for investment in other businesses. Profitable use of the positive cash flow was highly acclaimed by the industry and by financial institutions. In the recession positive cash flow decreased and it was found that the requirements for funds of their cash hungry businesses far outstripped their capacity to finance them. Thus there is no longer a move towards diversification to use the positive cash flow profitably. Indeed, the positive cash flow of contracting has substantially reduced and the equity taken by contractors in their projects has increased, thus focusing their attention on their core business.

The low fixed assets in contracting remain a characteristic of the industry. However in order for the larger construction companies to enter the newer markets available to them (see Chapter 5), they need more funding than previously and will probably have to concentrate more on their capital structure in the future. Moreover companies still need to create assets and seek a source of income separate from that from contracting. The type of diversification to achieve this is quite different from that of the 1980s (see Chapter 5).

Contracting companies are now less attractive to conglomerates because positive cash flow is seen as an unstable source of funds. Moreover it is suggested in this book that some family firms may have difficulty in surviving in that form because of the increased need for funds to participate with equity in projects.

10.8   PRICING POLICY

Similarly the chapter by Flanagan and Norman[21] on pricing policy is relevant in boom and recession although the practical effects of the application of theory are very different in the two circumstances.

The way in which contractors are obtaining a competitive advantage for particular projects by taking equity or by initiating the idea of the project, means that traditional price competition does not take place. In procuring projects in this way the contractor is laying out a considerable amount of finance in advance of receiving any payment and in the case of equity is investing in projects which have some degree of risk. On both counts the price obtained for the contracting work would be expected to be higher than under the traditional system. It may be that, on balance, they are not making much higher profits on these projects but they are attempting to ensure that they will obtain the contract and thus they reduce the level of competition. It is uncertain, however, whether the work additional to the tendering process is regarded as a general overhead or included in the total cost of the project.

This will have implications for the theory of pricing policy which is yet to be developed to cover such complex competitive situations. Indeed conventional theory is applicable to a rapidly decreasing portion of the workload of the contracting industry.

10.9   INTERNAL AND EXTERNAL MARKETS

The first chapter in the Theory Book by Cannon and Hillebrandt[22] discusses economic theories of the firm including transaction costs and the way in which these influence the organisation of firms towards internal provision of services as opposed to the purchase of services from the market. Firms have moved towards market supply since the middle 1980s. This was due first to the desire for flexibility and later in the recession to the wish to exercise choice. Table 10.1 shows the reasons for the movement to market supply over the last few years. For example contractors will choose the outside market in the decision to use supply and fix subcontractors as opposed to in-house capability because of lower price and less risk. But they will use the internal market if better control is vital. Thus the movement to market supply is due to a lower purchase price achievable during a recession and the lower risk and greater flexibility of buying in goods and services in the quantities, types and times required, which are not available during a boom because of shortage. During the recession firms have in some areas moved towards an internal market for what were central services eg training. This is probably more efficient in many respects but also reflects the reduced importance of these services during a recession. The internal market could still be used for services which head offices

Table 10.1   Reasons for movement to market supply

	Recession related			Happening anyway
	Outside market			Internal market
	Lower price	Less risk	Need for choice	Better control
Supply and fix subcontracting or in-house	√	√	x	√
Labour-only subcontracting or direct employment	√	√	x	na
Buy in managers or develop own	x	√	x	na
Buy in other services or in-house	√	√	√	√
Buy in training or in-house	x	√	√	√
Buy in materials or in-house	√	√	√	√

Notes: √ = relevant
x = not relevant
na = not applicable

were keen to promote by means of a centrally funded subsidy. Now in the recession the stress is on the individual businesses' decisions.

This movement towards market supply is not inconsistent with the view developed by Michael Ball[23] that the contracting industry operates essentially as merchants dealing in a portfolio of contracts and gaining the maximum advantage out of the conditions of commodity exchange in the purchase of inputs for production.

The conclusions of Buckley and Enderwick[24] in their chapter on Manpower Management in the Theory Book, that the weaknesses of subcontracting in manufacturing are attenuated in the construction industry and that subcontracting offers a low cost mode of organising work in the construction industry, are upheld by the field work in 1986 and also by the present study. Similar developments are taking place in management with a policy of buying-in managers when required increasingly being adopted. This is discussed further in Section 10.10 below. Buckley and Enderwick go on to say that 'labour-only subcontracting offers advantages in efficiency and control. The positive advantages of labour-only subcontracting have to be tempered by the social costs of failure to train and a possible reduction in safety'. All forms of subcontracting have persisted in boom and in recession and there seems little possibility of a future decrease. Chapter 9 (Section 9.2) contains a full discussion of this matter.

10.10 MANAGEMENT AND ORGANISATION STRUCTURE

A theoretical approach to the organisational structure of the construction company is outlined in Clark's[25] chapter in the Theory Book 'Social Technology and Structure'. He stresses the importance of ensuring that the structure of the organisation and its methods of communication are appropriate to the types of information which have to be used in the construction process. The operation of any group may be examined within the framework put forward. Crucial to the argument is that, as the inputs to the construction process become more stable, more uniform and better understood, as Clark maintains they did in the twenty years to 1986, the organisation at the centre would become more centralised and powerful and the site management less powerful. The 1986 study reported in the Industry Book did not find any movement towards better understood, more stable information in construction firms and there was no evidence that one type of organisational structure was more likely to lead to a profitable company than another. It is clear that the opposite from that postulated by Clark has in fact been the case. To some extent the individual inputs have become more variable, the professional and managerial expertise has become more diverse and the process now takes many more different forms. In the recession there has been a less structured situation. Moreover the general move has been towards decentralisation not centralisation.

Other theory and previous research have suggested that in uncertain and difficult times firms need to develop better integration combined with looser control in order to be responsive to change and opportunities. However as reported by Lansley and Quince,[26] in the face of change firms will often increase the degree of bureaucratization and control at the expense of integration. They may also fail to recognise the importance of new skills. There is evidence of both these extremes of action having taken place in the last recession.

The analysis of the present study supports the hypothesis that during a boom the organisational structure of companies becomes overmanned and inefficient. Control by top management becomes lax and the parts become laws unto themselves. During a recession the over-heavy management structure is slimmed down and although certain functions previously centralised are decentralised, the financial controls are actually strengthened. The companies studied have in many ways improved their management in the recession. Nevertheless the 'pit stop' theory, according to which in a recession the companies simply stop for minor repairs and replacements and continue fit for the rest of the race, does not hold water for the contracting industry. The companies have to do some drastic refitting, even ditching some parts previously regarded as vital, and are not for the most part as fit to go back into the race as they should be, especially for the long-term. For example, they are not training managers and their financial strength is impaired.

A pause of a certain duration or even a certain depth of fall in output could be said to have benefits for the health of companies and hence to fit the 'pit stop' theory. It would be interesting to try and define the depth and duration of recession which was not harmful in the long run and distinguish it from that which is harmful. The recession of the 1990s seems to have crossed the boundary to the harmful category.

One of the negative effects of the recession is the decline in training activities and low levels of recruitment of young people. Both contribute to a reduction in the potential skill level of the industry. There needs to be a better understanding of the effects of changes in workload on training and employment of manpower.

The chapter in the Theory Book by Male and Stocks[27] which essentially classified management structures holds in broad terms in boom and recession. There have however been some changes which have been prompted by the recession. Above all in terms of the Miles and Snow[28] classification most contractors would be classed as reactors or defenders in recession rather than in boom periods.

In Chapter 8 of the Industry Book attitudes of firms to management employment practices are discussed, especially recruitment, promotion and training. In the recession the strategy reported in this book is more concerned with redundancy than recruitment, providing continued employment rather than promotion and cutting back training rather than developing it.

A major change has been a steady progression towards the division of staff into core and disposable. While in the 1986 study most firms preferred to grow their own management, now an increasing number are relying on buying in staff when they require them and even using agency staff. Contracting professionals are seen as independent operators with many being mobile and self employed. This follows the change in manufacturing industry which began many years ago, of the demise of a 'job for life' and the expectation by senior executives of changing jobs several times in a career. In the course of this change and in response to the recession there has been a rapid reduction in senior ranks, who are more protected than junior ranks, by early retirement and of lower ranks by redundancy schemes. This is in keeping with the move towards contractors as merchants buying inputs as required (see Section 10.2).

Although a major reason for the decline of training has been the unwillingness or inability of companies to devote funds to it, another reason is the increased mobility of middle and senior management which reduces the long-term advantages to a firm of investment in training. Expenditure on training is likely to benefit the individual in enhancing his career prospects rather than the company which finances it.

These changes must affect the motivation of managers. Whereas at one time the long-term interests of the managers and the company were the same, now there could be considerable divergence with managers promoting behaviours which would enhance their personal reputation but which might or might not correspond with that best suited to the progress of the company. There is especially likely to be a clash between short-term and long-term goals. The self-interests of managers may gear the behaviour of the companies more to short-term rather than long-term success.

10.11   EFFECT OF RECESSION ON INNOVATION

The whole of this book is concerned with the effect of recession which was not mentioned in the previous two books. Clearly the settings of the earlier and the present research raises the issue of at what stage in the economic cycle are firms likely to be at their most flexible and able to change. Some work has been done on this in relation to innovation by Lansley[29] and van Duijn[30] who distinguish between process innovation and product innovation. Table 10.2 summarises their conclusions. In construction product innovation is at its peak in a period of recession and then fades as prosperity returns whereas process innovation is strongest in a period of decline and then ebbs as recovery develops. Manufacturing is somewhat similar as is shown by the table but con-

Table 10.2   Propensity to innovate in construction and manufacturing industry

	Recession	Recovery	Prosperity	Decline
Construction				
Product Innovation	++++	+++	+	+
Process Innovation	++	+	++	+++
Manufacturing Industry				
Product Innovation	+++	+++	+	+
Process Innovation	+++	+	++	++

Note: The more pluses the greater the likelihood that innovation will take place.
Source: based on Lansley, Peter, 'Organisational Innovation and Development' in Male, S.P. and Stocks, R.K, *Competitive Advantage in Construction*, (Oxford: Butterworth–Heinemann, 1991) and van Duijn J.J., 'Fluctuations in Innovation over Time' in Freeman, C., *Long Waves in the World Economy* (London: Frances Pinter, 1984).

struction firms will seek process innovations very much earlier in a period of decline than manufacturing industry, perhaps because the opportunities are greater and because efficiency improvements in contracting are more organisational and less dependent on plant and equipment. An example in construction of product innovation is involvement of companies in the earlier stages of a project. An example of process innovation in recession is improvement of financial budgeting and control. However, most examples of innovation tend to concern immediate relationships with the environment especially clients rather than the internal organisation.

Hillebrandt[31] regarded the stop-go period of the 1960s as more likely to have induced innovation than would have stability on the grounds that rapid technological change was produced in booms and consolidated during recessions.

10.12 CONCLUSION

Because social and business behaviour does not lend itself to experimentation it is important to study the effects of changes in the environment as they occur. This study has taken advantage of the recession in construction to study its effects on the behaviour of firms and to compare the situation with the earlier investigation of companies' strategies in a period of upturn. This presented an opportunity to investigate how well theory and the accepted wisdom of good strategies has stood up to changed circumstances.

Unfortunately there has been very little development of theory specifically in relation to the construction industry since the Theory Book was written. This is borne out by an analysis of the content of the journal *Construction Management and Economics*[32] from 1983 to 1992 which found that although much academic research in construction has contributed new insights and the ingredients for the development of new theory, often as the result of reviews, very little research (less than 5%) has been concerned with the development of theory.

It is clear from the brief assessments in this chapter of the value of theories and guidelines expounded in the first volume in this series that a fresh approach to some areas is required. Theories and guidelines should be generally applicable and should hold good for or be adapted to conditions of boom or recession. Areas where new hypotheses are needed at least for the construction industry, concern the importance and influence of transaction costs, the general effects of recession, portfolio management including the choice of markets in which to develop or shrink, diversification and pricing policy.

References

1. Hillebrandt, Patricia M. and Cannon, Jacqueline, *The Management of Construction Firms: Aspects of Theory* (London: Macmillan, 1989).
2. Hillebrandt, Patricia M. and Cannon, Jacqueline, *The Modern Construction Firm* (London: Macmillan, 1990).
3. For example: Mintzberg, Henry, *The Rise and Fall of Strategic Planning* (London: Prentice-Hall, 1994); Quinn, James, *Strategies for Change – Logical Incrementalism* (Homewood, Il: Richard D. Irwin, 1980): and Ohmae, Kenichi, *The Mind of the Strategist: The Art of Japanese Business* (New York: McGraw-Hill, 1982).
4. Ramsay, William, 'Business Objectives and Strategy' in Hillebrandt and Cannon (1989) *op.cit.*
5. Porter, Michael, *Competitive Strategy: Techniques for Analyzing Industries and Competitors* (New York: The Free Press, 1980); and Porter, Michael, *Competitive Advantage: Creating and Sustaining Superior Performance* (New York: The Free Press, 1980).
6. Slatter, Stuart, St P., *Corporate Recovery – A Guide to Turnaround Management,* (Harmondsworth: Penguin, 1984).
7. Harrigan, Kathryn Rudi, *Strategies for Defining Businesses* (Lexington, MA: Lexington Books–D.C. Heath, 1980).
8. Ramsay, William, *op. cit.*
9. McKinsey, *New Game Strategies,* McKinsey Staff Paper (New York: McKinsey, 1980).
10. Ramsay, William, *op. cit.*
11. Quinn, James, *op. cit.*
12. Mintzberg, Henry, *op. cit.*
13. Stacey, Ralph D., *Dynamic Strategic Management for the 1990s* (London: Kogan Page, 1990).
14. Peters, Tom and Waterman, Robert, *In Search of Excellence* (New York: Harper & Row, 1982).
15. Langford, D.A. and Male, S.P., *Strategic Management in Construction,* (Aldershot: Gower, 1991).
16. Stacey, Ralph, *op. cit.*
17. Cannon, Jacqueline and Hillebrandt, Patricia M., 'Diversification' in Hillebrandt and Cannon (1989), *op. cit.*
18. Seymour, Howard, 'International Contracting' in Hillebrandt and Cannon (1989), *op. cit.*

19. Cannon, Jacqueline and Hillebrandt, Patricia M., 'Theories of the Firm' in Hillebrandt and Cannon (1989), *op. cit.*

20. Cannon, Jacqueline and Hillebrandt, Patricia M., 'Financial Strategy' in Hillebrandt and Cannon (1989), *op. cit.*

21. Flanagan, Roger, and Norman, George, 'Pricing Policy' in Hillebrandt and Cannon (1989), *op. cit.*

22. Seymour, Howard, *op. cit.*

23. Ball, Michael, *Rebuilding Construction* (London: Routledge, 1988).

24. Buckley, Peter J. and Enderwick, Peter, 'Manpower Management' in Hillebrandt and Cannon, (1989) *op. cit.*

25. Clark, Peter, 'Social Technology and Structure' in Hillebrandt and Cannon (1989) *op. cit.*

26. Lansley, Peter and Quince, Thelma, 'Organisational Responses to a Major Recession', *Construction Papers,* Vol. 1, No. 2, 1981, pp. 5–16.

27. Male, Steven and Stocks, Robert, 'Managers and the Organisation' in Hillebrandt and Cannon (1989) *op. cit.*

28. Miles, R.E., Snow, C.C., Meyer, A.D. and Coleman, H.J.,'Organisational Strategy, Structure and Process', *Academy of Management Review,* July 1978.

29. Lansley, Peter, 'Organisational Innovation and Development' in Male, S.P. and Stocks, R.K. *Competitive Advantage in Construction* (Oxford: Butterworth–Heinemann, 1991).

30. van Duijn, J.J., 'Fluctuations in Innovations Over Time' in Freeman, C., *Long Waves in the World Economy* (London, Frances Pinter, 1984).

31. Hillebrandt, Patricia, 'The Capacity of the Construction Industry' in Turin, D.A. (ed). *Aspects of the Economics of Construction* (London: Godwin, 1975).

32. Betts, Martin and Lansley, Peter, 'Construction Management and Economics: A review of the first ten years', *Construction Management and Economics*, Vol. 11, No. 4, 1993, pp. 221–45.

Appendix 1

CHANGES IN ACCOUNTING RULES

The new accounting standard, FRS3, requires the adoption of accounting rules which differ from those previously followed. The changes are complex. However the following observations highlight some important points.

(a) In previous years profits and losses on the sale of fixed assets carried at valuation have been included in the profit and loss account based on the difference between proceeds and depreciated historical costs.

(b) In previous years certain profits and losses were treated as extraordinary items in accordance with standard accounting practice at that time. Such profits or losses are now included within operating profit or treated as exceptional items and shown after operating profit, but before interest, in accordance with the new accounting standard.

(c) In previous years earnings per share have been calculated on the figure for profit after taxation, minority interests and preference dividends, but before extraordinary items. Under the new accounting standard earnings per share are based on profit after taxation, minority interests, preference dividends and extraordinary items.

EXCEPTIONAL ITEMS

This is a UK expression for those items in a profit and loss account that are written within the normal activities of the business, but are of unusual size. The treatment for these, as laid down in accounting standards (SSAP 6), is to disclose them separately in the profit and loss account or the notes to it. Such items are to be distinguished from extraordinary items.

EXTRAORDINARY ITEMS

These are gains or losses which are outside the normal activities of the business, are of significant size, and are not expected to recur. An example would be the gain on the sale of a significant part of a business. The inclusion of such items would distort a view of 'sustainable' profit. On the other hand, the items did happen in the year, so there is an argument for including them. Fortunately it is possible both to include and to exclude them, by showing profits before and profits after extraordinary items. For the purposes of the calculation of earnings per share, the extraordinary items are excluded.

The rules for extraordinary items are to be found in accounting standards: SSAP 6 in the UK, and APB 30 in the USA. There are, however, great problems in defining exactly what an extraordinary item is. Companies can make their earnings figures better by attempting to classify as many losses (but as few gains) as possible as extraordinary. Indeed, one UK technical partner of an accounting firm has suggested that the only workable accounting standard would be for such losses to be treated as extraordinary items and such gains to be treated as exceptional items (the latter are included in normal profit).

Appendix 2

LOCATION OF DISCUSSION OF TOPICS IN THE THREE BOOKS

Section	Topic	Theory Book Chapter	Industry Book Chapter	This Volume Chapter
10.2	Strategy	2	2,3	3,4,5,6,8,10
10.3	Market Portfolios	2	2,3	4,5,8
10.4	Corporate Planning	2	2	6,10
10.5	Diversification	3	3	4,5,8,10
10.6	International Contracting	4	6	4,5,8,10
10.7	Financial Strategy	5	4	3,10
10.8	Pricing Policy	9	5	3,10
10.9	Internal and External Markets	1,8	97,9,10	
10.10	Management and Organisation Structure	6,7,8,9	5,7,8,9	6,7,8,10
10.11	Effects of Recession	–	–	All

PRINCIPAL CONTENTS OF THE COMPANION VOLUME, *THE MANAGEMENT OF CONSTRUCTION FIRMS: ASPECTS OF THEORY*

1. Theories of the Firm
   Jacqueline Cannon and Patricia M. Hillebrandt
2. Business Objectives and Strategy
   William Ramsay
3. Diversification
   Jacqueline Cannon and Patricia M. Hillebrandt
4. International Contracting
   Howard Seymour
5. Financial Strategy
   Jacqueline Cannon and Patricia M. Hillebrandt
6. Social Technology and Structure
   Peter Clark
7. Managers and the Organisation
   Steven Male and Robert Stocks
8. Manpower Management
   Peter J. Buckley and Peter Enderwick
9. Pricing Policy
   Roger Flanagan and George Norman

PRINCIPAL CONTENTS OF THE COMPANION VOLUME, *THE MODERN CONSTRUCTION FIRM*

PART I   BACKGROUND
 1 The Industry Yesterday and Today

PART II   OVERALL STRATEGY OF LARGE FIRMS
 2 Objectives and Strategy of Firms
 3 Growth and Diversification
 4 Financial Policy

PART III   IMPLEMENTATION OF STRATEGY
 5 Marketing and Bidding Policy
 6 International Policy
 7 Structure and Organisation

PART IV   HUMAN RESOURCES
 8 The Management Resource
 9 Manpower Management and Subcontracting

PART V   CONCLUSION
10 Conclusions

Subject Index

Accounting rules, changes in 25–34
  passim, 173–4
Acquisitions, as response to recession
  78, 127
Assets
  disposal of 32, 38, 41–2, 63–4,
    122, 124, 133, 149
  future need for 95, 162–3
  1986 increase 124
  70 large companies 25, 26, 28
  value of 52
  writing down values 25, 29–30,
    38, 41–2

Balance sheets
  off balance sheet transactions 40
  70 large companies 25–30
  survey companies 43, 45, 52, 121
Bank of England 11, 38
Bankruptcies 16
Banks 7, 18, 37–43 *passim*, 46–7,
  59–60, 94, 95, 139–40
Bidding policy, in response to
  recession 78
Bonding 37, 40, 57–8
  and cash flow 140
Borrowings 25, 37, 38, 46, 122, 133
Boston Matrix 150–2
British Standard Institution Quality
  Assurance Standard BS5750
  82
Builders' merchants 63
Building, *passim*, *notably* xxii, 14,
  64
Building and civil engineering
  passim, *notably* xxii, 64
Building, public 20–1
Building services xxii, 14

Cadbury Report 93, 97, 98, 107
Capacity, present overcapacity
  139–41

Capital expenditure, control of 59
Capital structure 37–46
Cash flow 16, 37, 41, 46, 48, 52–7,
  123, 124–5, 128, 134, 139–40,
  162
  in contracting 52–4
  in housing 54–5
  in mining and minerals 56–7
  in property 55–6
  monitoring 58
Channel Tunnel 12, 21, 23
Civil engineering xxii, 14, 64,
  see also infrastructure
Client confidence 40, 61
Commercial construction 3, 17–20,
  68–9
  orders 13
  output 13, 19
  recession 12, 17–20
  see also property
Communications 22
Company finance *see* financial
  matters, financial control
Company management
  centralisation *v.* decentralisation
    99–101
  and corporate planning 102–7
  executive committees 98–9
  problems 95–6
  relevance of theory 165–8
  size and composition of boards
    97–9
  see also company planning,
    managers
Company objectives 38–9, 46,
  123–8
  change 1986 to 1994 123–8
  relevance of theory 149
Company organisation 95–102, 121
  change 1986 to 1994 130–1
  relevance of theory 165–8
  type of company 93–5

Company planning   73–4, 102–7,
    131
  contractors' approach   158
  implementation of plans   106–7,
    159
  relevance of theory   156–9
Company strategy, relevance of
    theory   148
Company structure   95–101, 121
  change 1986 to 1994   130–1
  relevance of theory   165–6
Competitive advantage   148
Construction management   85
Construction materials   xxii, 3, 4
Construction output   5–23 *passim*
Construction process
  changes 10–11
  and large contractors   31
Contract duration   66, 85
Contract size   48, 65–6
Contracting   *passim, notably*   3, 4,
    8, 14, 42, 65–6
  as core business   64
  cash flow   52–4
  as market   65–6
  and new types of marketing
    85–6, 133
  profits   46, 49, 65
  and 70 large companies   25, 30–4
  survey companies   45–9 *passim,*
    64–6, 85–6, 133
  turnover   39, 45, 65–6
  see also European links
Contractors' links between
    companies   *see* European links
Core businesses
  focus on   63–4, 121, 122, 124
  marketing in 77
  nature of   64, 150
Corporate   *see* company
Costs
  control   37, 58–9, 101, 122
  cutting   37, 38, 44, 59, 110–12
Credit   37, 58

Debt/equity ratio   *see* gearing

Debts   59–60
  conversion to equity   38, 42
  rescheduling   38, 42, 122
Decentralisation and centralisation
    99–100
Design and build   82–4, 130
  novated   84
Differentiation of product
  change 1986 to 1994   129–30
  and theory   149
Diversification   38, 63–5, 88–91,
    124, 160, 162–3
  new forms of   88–91, 125–6
  present relevance   125, 160
  relevance of theory   159–60
Dividends   37, 38, 49–50, 94, 122

Educational building   20–1
Electrical engineering   63
Employment   9, 38, 121–2
  in construction   14, 59; manager
    110–15; operative   141–3;
    practices   132, 167
Energy   12
Environment, operating for firms   3,
    4, 6–11
Equity in projects   78, 86, 125, 130,
    140
  see also finance for projects
European links   9, 58, 71
  and possible mergers   140
European Quality Registration   82
European Union
  directives   9–10, 144–5
  funding   9
  obtaining contracts   71
Exceptional items
  changes in treatment   173
  70 large companies   25–6, 29–30,
    33,
  survey companies   40–1
Extraordinary items, changes in
    accounting rules   173–4

Family firms   xxii, 43–4, 49, 95,
    141
Financial control   58–9, 101, 149

Financial matters
  policies 1986 and 1994 128–30
  relevance of theory 162–3
  70 large companies 25–34
  survey companies 37–61
Finance for projects 40, 80, 85–8,
  126, 130, 140
Foreign companies xxii, 25

Gas 22
Gearing
  need to reduce 40
  70 large companies 25, 29
  survey companies 38–41, 45, 68,
  128
Geographical areas of operation
  Africa 73; Nigeria 73,
    Zimbabwe 73
  Asia 72; Kazakhstan 72;
    Turkey 72; Turkmenistan
    72
  Australia 73
  Criteria 70
  Europe 71–2; Czech Rep. 72;,
    East Germany 72; Poland
    72; Slovak Rep. 72
  Far East 10, 70–1; Cambodia
    70; China 70; Hong Kong
    70; Indonesia 70; Malaysia
    71; Thailand 70; Vietnam
    70
  Middle East 10, 71; Abu Dhabi
    71; Dubai 71
  North America 72–3; Canada
    73; USA 72
  South America 73
  UK: commercial work 17–19;
    housing 16–18;
    infrastructure 19, 23,
    regions 24
  see also regional offices
Government – role in construction
  7, 8
Gross domestic product (GDP) 6
Growth, as company objective 38,
  124, 126, 127

Health, buildings 20–1

Housing 14–17, 66–8
  acquisition of businesses 68
  affordability 12, 14
  cash flow 54–5
  collapse of market 25, 39, 44, 66
  as core business 64
  developers 67
  flexibility 49
  means of selling 66–7
  orders 13, 16
  output 12–17 *passim*, 66–8
  prices 46, 66
  private 14–17, 20–1
  profits 46, 66
  public 20–1
  recession 12–17 *passim*, 66–8
  sale of business 68
  starts 16, 18, 20–1
  and top 70 companies 30, 32
Housing Associations 3, 17, 20

Industrial building 12
  orders 13
  output 13
Information technology (IT) xix, 7
Infrastructure 12, 21–3
  in the Far East 71
  output 13, 14, 18, 21
  orders 13, 21
  public and private 23
Innovation, effect of recession on
  168–9
Interest rates 11, 12, 14, 16, 18, 20,
  24, 68
  interest changes 40
Internal and external markets,
  relevance of theory 163–5
International construction 10, 32,
  69–73, 80
  increase in recession 67–70, 86,
  121–3
  management for 99, 114–15
  markets 10, 69–73, 78
  relevance of theory 161–2
  type of business 70
  see also geographical areas of
    operation

Interviews   xxi–xxiii

Labour-only subcontracting   141–2,
   165
Land
   banks   15, 55, 69
   price   15–16
   purchase and payment   44–5,
      66–8
   recycled   68
   sales   39
   transactions   16
   writing down of value   25, 33, 39,
      67
Latham Report   8, 10–11, 145
Lending
   to construction companies   11, 13
   to property companies   11, 13
Losses   *see* profits

Managers   109–19
Management contracting   84–5
Management control   133, 134
Management resource   109–19
   characteristics   113–5
   development   110
   French and German managers   115
   management development
      117–19, 131–2
   permanent versus contract
      112–13
   reduction in numbers employed
      110–12
   training   110, 115–17, 131–2
   type of managers   109–10
Manufacturing output   6–7
Marketing   63–76, 77–91, 129
   advantage of public companies   94
   increased attention to   121
   international   70–3
   manager   75–6
   of contracting services   77–91;
      abroad   78, 80 (*see also*
      international construction);
      creating demand   70, 85–6,
      130; design and build, etc.
      82–5, 30; diversification and

specialisation   88–91;
   finance of projects   70, 85–6,
   130; forward extension of
   project   85; quality   82;
   regional penetration   78–9
policy   73–6, 122, 130, 133,
   149–50
role of board and executives   76,
   133
Markets   63–76, 77–91 *passim*,
   126
   change 1986 to 1994   129
   relevance of theory   150–6
Materials   xxii
   and 70 large companies   30, 32
   see also minerals
Mechanical engineering   63
Mergers   122, 139–40
   see also takeovers
Minerals   xxii, 3, 4, 63, 64, 69
   as core business   64, 69
   cash flow   56–7
   and 70 large companies   30
   survey companies   56–7, 69
Mining
   see minerals
Monetary policy   11, 14, 23–4
Mortgages
   interest rates   11, 12
   multiple   14
   tax relief   14, 66

Offices   3, 18, 19
   boom   17
   recession   12
   see also commercial construction
Operatives   141–3
Orders, general   24
Output   5–23 *passim*, 37

Planning
   see company planning
Plant and equipment   63
   1986 market   124
Portfolio of businesses   129
   relevance of theory   150–6
   see also markets

Prices 122
  of labour 46, 48
  of materials 46, 48
  of plant 48
  relevance of theory 163
  tender *see* tender prices
Price/earnings (ratio) (PE) 140
Private companies 61, 94
  see also family firms
Private finance initiative 8, 87–8
Privatisation 7, 22
Private sector
  housing xxii, 3, 9, 14–17
  output 8, 13
  orders 13
Process engineering xxii, 30, 64
Profits
  margins 24
  objective 126, 128
  70 large companies 25, 30
  survey companies 37–9, 45,
    46–9, 50, 123–4, 128, 134
Property
  boom 17–18
  as core business 64, 69
  as market 68–9
  cash flow 55–6
  collapse of market 12, 17–20, 24,
    25
  development – nature of
    participants 3, 55–6
  profits 46
  sale of assets 68–9
  70 large companies 30, 32, 33
  writing down values 39, 69
  see also commercial construction
Public limited companies xxii,
  93
  advantages and disadvantages
    94–5
Public sector
  building 20–1
  clients 7
  output 8
  see also infrastructure

Quality 82

Railways 22
Receivership, companies in
  80–2
Recession in construction *passim,*
  notably 11–12, 77–8
  and efficiency 101, 132, 166
  and innovation 168–9
  major disadvantages for industry
    24
  response in contracting and UK
    industry 77–8, 121–2
Redundancy 59, 111–12
  costs 40, 111
Regional offices 38, 59, 78–9,
  100–1, 123
  advantages of 78–9
  control of 79
  margins 79
Regional variations *see*
  geographical areas of operations
Regulatory framework 143–5
Repair and maintenance 12
Research 8
Retailing 19, 20
Retail Price Index (RPI) 11, 15
Retirement, early 111
Return on capital employed 49
Rights issues 38, 43, 49, 67, 122,
  127, 139
Risk 3, 48, 124, 159
  influencing projects 87–8
Roads 22, 23

Sewerage 7, 22, 23
Share values 37, 49, 50–52, 94, 124
Society, gains in recession 24
Specialisation 88–91, 124
Standards 9
Stock Exchange 37, 38, 40, 43, 49,
  59–61, 93–4, 140
Structure of companies *see*
  company structure
Structure of industry 4, 6, 31–2,
  65–6
Survey
  comparison with previous survey
    121–32

Survey—*continued*
  type of company xxii, 93–5

Takeover 50, 52, 61, 80–1, 122, 140
Technological change 9
Tender prices 46, 47–8, 65, 78, 163
Theory – towards redevelopment
  148–70
  corporate planning 156–9
  diversification 159–61
  effect of recession on innovation
    168–9
  financial strategy 162–3
  internal and external markets
    163–5
  international contracting 161–2
  management and structure 165–8
  market portfolios 150–6
  pricing policy 163
  strategy 148–50

Training 7, 8, 59, 121, 166–7
  managers 110, 115–7
  operatives 142–3
Transaction costs *see* internal and
  external markets
Transfer of Undertaking (Protection
  of Employment) Regulations
  1981 (TUPE) 80–1
Turnover
  80 top companies 26–8
  70 large companies 25, 30–4
  survey companies 39, 45,
    65–6

Value added tax (VAT) 68
Value engineering 82
Value management 82

Water 7, 12, 22, 23

Index of Names

Akintoye, A.   83, 91
Alfred McAlpine plc   *see* McAlpine (Alfred) plc
Allen plc   26
AMEC plc   26
Amey Holdings plc   26

Balfour Beatty Ltd   xvii, 26, 41, 45
Ball, M   165, 171
Barratt Developments plc   26
Beazer Homes plc   26
Bellway plc   26
Bellwinch plc   26
Berkeley Group plc   26
Betts, M.   171
Birse Group plc   26
Biwater Ltd   26
Bloor Holdings Ltd   26
Boot (Henry) & Sons plc   xvii, 26, 41, 45
Bovis Construction Ltd   xvii, 26, 41, 45
Bovis Homes Ltd   26
Bryant Group   26
Buckley, P.   165, 171
Building Employers Confederation (BEC)   xix, 10

Cadbury, Sir Adrian   93, 97, 98, 107
Cala plc   26
Cannon, J.   xxi, xxiii, 34, 107, 135, 159, 162, 163, 170, 171
Carter (R.G.) Holdings Ltd   26
Charles Church Developments plc   26
Chartered Institute of Building (CIOB)   xix, 60
Clark, P.   165, 171
Clugsten Group plc   26
Coleman, H.J.   171
Construction Forecasting and Research Ltd (CFR)   xvii, xix, 61

Construction Industry Council (CIC)   xix, 10
Construction Industry Employers Council (CIEC)   xix, 10
Construction Industry Training Board (CITB)   xix, 143
Construction Liaison Group   10
Coopers & Lybrand   61
Costain Group plc   xvii, 26 41, 45, 52
Countryside Properties plc   26
Crest Nicholson plc   26
Croudace Ltd   26

Davis Langdon & Everest   46
Department of the Environment (DoE)   xix, 8–9, 30, 145
Department of Social Security   142
Donelon Tyson plc   26
Duijn J.J. van   168, 171

EBC Group plc   26
Eleco Holdings plc   26
Enderwick, P   165, 171
Engineering and Physical Sciences Research Council   xvii
European Institute of Business Administration (INSEAD)   xix, 116
Eve Group plc   26
Export Credit Guarantee Department (ECGD)   xix, 70

Federation of Civil Engineering Contractors (FCEC)   xix, 10
Fitzpatrick plc   26
Flanagan, R.   163, 171

GA Holdings Ltd   26
Galliford plc   xvii, 26, 41, 45
General Electric   152
General Surety and Guarantee Co. Ltd (1994)   58

George Wimpey plc   *see* Wimpey
    (George) plc
Geroski, P.   37, 61, 64, 76, 77, 91,
    121, 135
Gleeson (MJ) Group plc   26
Green, S.D.   82, 91
Gregg, P.   37, 61, 64, 76, 77, 91,
    121, 135

Harrigan, K.R.   149, 170
Harvard Business School   116
Haymills Holdings Ltd   26
Henry Boot & Sons plc   *see* Boot
    (Henry) & Sons plc
Higgs & Hill plc   xvii, 26, 41, 45
Hillebrandt, P.M.   xxi, xxiii, 34,
    107, 135, 159, 162, 163, 169,
    170, 171

Inland Revenue   142
International Labour Office (ILO)
    xix

Jackson Group plc   26
Jarvis, J. & Sons plc   26
John Laing plc   *see* Laing (John) plc
John Mowlem & Co plc   *see*
    Mowlem (John) plc
Johnston Group plc   26
Joint Forecasting Committee for the
    Construction Industries   61
Joy, C.   xvii

Keepmoat Holdings Ltd   26
Keller Group   27
Kier Group plc   xvii, 27, 41, 45
Kyle Stewart Ltd   xvii

Laing, (John) plc   xvii, 27, 41, 45
Langford, D.A.   159, 170
Lansley, P.   107, 135, 166, 168, 171
Latham, Sir Michael   8, 10, 11, 24,
    145, 146
Longley (James) Holdings Ltd   27
Lighthill, J.   110, 119
London Business School   116
London Underground   58

Lovell (Y.J.) Holdings plc   xvii, 27,
    41, 45

McKinsey   152–3, 170
Male, S.P.   159, 167, 170, 171
Mansell (R.) Ltd   27
Maunders (John) Group plc   27
May Gurney Group   27
MBD   83, 91
McAlpine (Alfred) plc   27
McCarthy & Stone plc   27
Meikle, J.   xvii
Meyer A.D.   171
Miles, R.E.   167, 171
Miller Group Ltd   xvii, 27, 41, 45
Mintzberg, H.   157, 159, 170
Ministry of Defence   89
Morrison Construction Ltd   27
Morton, Alastair   88
Mowlem (John) & Co. plc   xvii, 27,
    41, 45

National Economic Development
    Office (NEDO)   xix, 44
Newarthill plc   27
Norman, G.   163, 171
Norwest Holst Ltd   27

Ohmae, K.   170
Osborne (Geoffrey) Ltd   27

Persimmon plc   27
Peters, T.   159, 170
Pochin's plc   27
Porter, M.   148, 159, 170
Property Services Agency   89
Prowting plc   27

Quince, T.   107, 135
Quinn, J.   157, 170

Raine Industries plc   27
Ramsay, W.   148–50 *passim*,
    156–7, 170
Redrow Group Ltd   27
Roberts (Thomas) West Ltd.   27
Roland Bardsley (Builders) Ltd   27

Seddon Group Ltd   27
Seymour, H.   161, 170, 171
Shanks & McEwan plc   27
Shepherd Building Group Ltd   27
Simms, N.I.   xv–xvi
Simons Group Ltd   27
Slatter, S. St P.   149, 170
Snow, C.C.   167, 171
Stacey, R.D.   158, 159, 170
Stocks, R.   167, 171
Sunley Turriff Holdings Ltd   27

Tarmac plc   xvi, xvii, 27, 41, 45
Tay Homes plc   27
Taylor Woodrow plc   xvii, 27, 41,
    45
Tilbury Douglas Ltd   27
Trafalgar House plc   27, 52, 58
Try Group plc   xvii, 27, 41, 45
Turin, D.A.   171

Union of Construction and A[
    Trades and Technicians
    (UCATT)   xix, 142
United Nations (UN)   xix,

Wain Group plc   27
Ward Holdings plc   27
Waterman, R.   159, 170
Wates Building Group I
Westbury plc   27
Willmot Dixon Ltd   x
Wilson Bowden plc
Wilson Connolly plc
    45
Wiltshier plc   28
Wimpey (George) [
    45

Y.J. Lovell Holdi
    (Y.J.) Holdi

Seddon Group Ltd   27
Seymour, H.   161, 170, 171
Shanks & McEwan plc   27
Shepherd Building Group Ltd   27
Simms, N.I.   xv–xvi
Simons Group Ltd   27
Slatter, S. St P.   149, 170
Snow, C.C.   167, 171
Stacey, R.D.   158, 159, 170
Stocks, R.   167, 171
Sunley Turriff Holdings Ltd   27

Tarmac plc   xvi, xvii, 27, 41, 45
Tay Homes plc   27
Taylor Woodrow plc   xvii, 27, 41, 45
Tilbury Douglas Ltd   27
Trafalgar House plc   27, 52, 58
Try Group plc   xvii, 27, 41, 45
Turin, D.A.   171

Union of Construction and Allied
   Trades and Technicians
   (UCATT)   xix, 142
United Nations (UN)   xix, 70

Wain Group plc   27
Ward Holdings plc   27
Waterman, R.   159, 170
Wates Building Group Ltd   27
Westbury plc   27
Willmot Dixon Ltd   xvii, 28, 41, 45
Wilson Bowden plc   27
Wilson Connolly plc   xvii, 28, 41, 45
Wiltshier plc   28
Wimpey (George) plc   xvii, 28, 41, 45

Y.J. Lovell Holdings plc   *see* Lovell
   (Y.J.) Holdings plc